Vegetarian
Baby

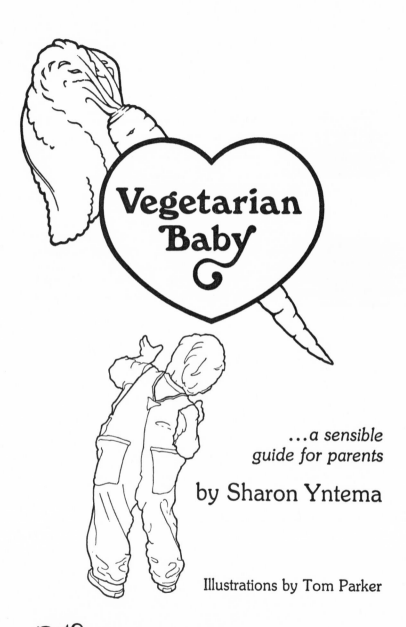

Vegetarian Baby

*...a sensible
guide for parents*

by Sharon Yntema

Illustrations by Tom Parker

 McBooks Press • Ithaca, New York

The author and publisher believe that this book outlines an excellent regimen for raising a healthy baby. However, they cannot accept any responsibility for the health of your child should any problems arise. Every child has individual nutritional needs. While using the information in this book you should consult with your pediatrician or public health nurse about your child's individual requirements.

Copyright © 1980 Sharon Kathryn Yntema

Cover design by Tom Parker
Book design by Mary A. Scott
Typesetting by Strehle's Computerized Typesetting
Back cover photograph by Kathy Morris

Library of Congress Cataloging in Publication Data

Yntema, Sharon Kathryn, 1951-
   Vegetarian baby.

   Bibliography: p.
   Includes index.
   1. Infants—Nutrition. 2. Vegetarianism.
3. Baby foods. I. Title.
RJ216.Y57   649'.3   79-24623
ISBN 0-935526-01-3
ISBN 0-935526-02-1 pbk.

This book is distributed to the book trade by The Crossing Press, Trumansburg, N.Y. 14886. Individuals may order this book from bookstores or directly from The Crossing Press. Please include $1.00 postage and handling with mail orders.

Printed in the United States of America

2 4 6 8 9 7 5 3 1

For Nikolas

About the Author

Sharon Kathryn Yntema was born in Detroit, Michigan, in 1951. She grew up in the U.S. Virgin Islands, where she was first introduced to the vegetarian way of life. She received a B.A. in psychology from Earlham College in Indiana and a M.A. in early childhood special education from George Washington University in Washington, D.C. Prior to the birth of her son in April of 1978, she worked as a child development specialist at the Day Care and Development Council of Tompkins County in Ithaca, NY. Still in Ithaca, she is now raising her son and working part-time as a bookseller.

` Thanks. . .

. . .to Alex Skutt, my publisher, who has been a friend and strong advocate of writing this book because he believes it is worthwhile and important.

. . .to Bill Kehoe and Katharyn Machan Aal, who edited this book, and Mary Scott, who designed it.

. . .to Tom Parker, for his enthusiasm about this book and his impressive artistic skills.

. . .to Phil Tomlinson, for his invaluable aid especially with parent interviews.

. . .to Elaina Jeddery and Shari Jackson, for their extensive typing.

. . .to Ann Lapinsky, for her contribution to the nutritional information in this book.

. . .to Pamela Peirce, for her generosity in allowing me to reprint her article, "Vegetarianism and Pregnancy."

. . .to all of the vegetarian parents and friends who were willing to give time to help me decide what parents most needed to know.

. . .to all of the people, too numerous to mention individually, but each one special, who gave me encouragement along the way.

And finally, a thank you to my son Nikolas, who is growing up healthy and happy, proving that this book is worth all the energy it took to write.

Table of Contents

Introduction

*"The time we take to be thoughtful
about how we live is extra time for living
better."*

Laurel's Kitchen

When I was approaching adolescence, my mother began to introduce brown rice into our main meals. Soy grits replaced hamburger meat in our spaghetti sauce. Brewer's yeast flavored our orange juice, gagging me, but delighting my baby brother who knew no different. We still ate meat, but meatless meals appeared more often. Walnut Acres sent us shipments of "health foods" that weren't available where we lived; I remember the excitement when one of these packages would arrive, filled with interesting foods I still did not recognize.

During the time I was in college, vegetarianism grew in popularity. It had the aura of an esoteric secret being revealed. To most of us, it meant adding brown rice and sprouts and homemade bread to our diets and removing meat. I ate with friends off campus who were vegetarians and I enjoyed those meals much more than I did the standard college fare. I knew the difference well because I worked in the school cafeteria, serving meat meals, but leaving as soon as my shift was over to eat my vegetarian meal. I lived with meat eaters during my last two years in college, and had to pay only a small portion of the weekly budget since meat comprised the major cost of meals. This economic advantage continued after college. I lived in cooperatives for several years, and I believe I paid about one-third the amount paid by the meat eaters.

It wasn't until I was pregnant that I began to realize how little I really knew about vegetarian nutrition. Despite this lack of knowledge, I was healthy, partly because my mother had ingrained in me some healthy eating patterns from such an early age.

My husband has been a much stricter vegetarian than I for many years. While I eat dairy products and, occasionally, seafood, he prefers to eat few dairy products and eggs, and no meat. While I was pregnant, we decided that we wanted to raise our baby as a vegetarian, and to learn enough about nutrition so that we would know what we were doing. We knew that raising a child as a vegetarian was not a venture anyone should undertake in ignorance.

As I studied vegetarian nutrition, I found that the specific needs of babies were often ignored in books, or, at best, mentioned only briefly. There was no one book that answered all my questions. This omission nagged me as I proceeded to raise my vegetarian baby.

However, I became knowledgeable in a number of necessary areas through extensive reading and wanted to share my information with other parents. I was invited to give a workshop on the subject of feeding babies meatless meals. The response from this workshop and from informal conversations with other parents confirmed my conclusion that there was a need for a handbook on vegetarian nutrition and cooking for babies.

The first reading I did was an exploration of other vegetarian cultures, searching for clues as to what their people fed their babies and why. This reading also gave me confidence that our decision to raise our baby as a vegetarian was the wisest one. I have described in Chapter One what I learned from vegetarian societies throughout the world.

I must have seen the acronym "RDA" a million times on cereal boxes if nowhere else, but I had no idea how these Recommended Dietary Allowances were arrived at, or how a baby's requirements might differ from an adult's. I found the most recent (1974) booklet published by the National Academy of Sciences, which explains how the RDA's were developed and describes the research that determined these allowances. I was surprised to find out that even this prestigious group does not believe there are any absolutes in the field of nutrition; this lack of absolutes results in allowances for some nutrients being much higher or lower than might be right for any one individual. I put together the National Academy's recommendations with the nutrition information for vegetarians currently available. I have summarized in Chapter Two the information applicable to a vegetarian baby.

The information that I read concerning the nutrition of pregnant and nursing mothers sometimes seemed too impersonal, even though I knew it was a very essential part of raising a vegetarian baby. I felt that I understood this information much more clearly when I talked with other parents who had already had a baby or babies and who were raising healthy vegetarian children. Every parent had a unique story to share. In Chapter Three I have included some of these stories along with essential information about nutrition especially for pregnant and lactating mothers.

My academic background is in child development, so naturally I am very interested in the relationship between the social and physiological aspects of eating. I also wanted to know answers to questions such as "When can you feed a baby tofu?" and "Why is a baby ready for beans at around ten months of age, but not before?" The writing of Chapter Four, "Development and Diet," was especially enjoyable. I felt that I was sorting out pieces of a biological puzzle.

I believe that knowing more about the foods you eat will make eating them more enjoyable. Respecting these natural gifts and the utensils that you use to prepare them is as important as any other aspect of feeding a baby. Chapter Five describes food preparation in its various aspects.

The final chapter of this book is the recipe section. I have included all of the kinds of recipes that I have actually tried with my son. It is divided according to age group because, naturally, some foods are better suited to fourteen-month -olds than to seven-month-olds. My son was usually very willing to experiment along with me. I have developed complete meals rather than individual dishes, for the most part, so that parents will not have to spend a lot of extra time figuring out how to make a well-balanced meal. I do expect that parents will develop many of their own recipes, based on the ones offered here.

I hope that this book as a whole will free vegetarian parents from any hesitations created by the meat-eating culture surrounding us. All new parents experience fears that they may not be doing the best for their children, whether it be in the area of discipline, education, or feeding. Many parents simply do not trust themselves to know intuitively what is best. This attitude is not odd in a culture such as ours which separates families and encourages the nuclear family to solve all its problems alone. Our culture offers very little support for new parents, providing no replacement for the wisdom of grandparents and other members in an extended family. Often there are no grandparents nearby to offer advice, and even if there are, many new parents feel that advice from another generation is an intrusion. Today, when the people of childbearing age in the United States are seriously adopting lifestyles different from those of their parents, this alienation is heightened.

Very few vegetarians whom I know have parents who are or were vegetarians, and while my friends' parents tolerate this difference, there is no move on their part to experiment with this approach to eating. Therefore, grandparents remain ignorant of vegetarian nutritional principles and have little to offer their children or grandchildren in this important area.

Most children who grow up eating meat learn their habits from their parents, who simply pass on the meat-eating tradition with which they themselves grew up. New vegetarians don't have inherited traditions to give their children; they must create their own. A new vegetarian is like an adult learning a second language. Children can speak their native language with ease and fluency by the time they are five years old; they have grown up hearing and speaking nothing else. An adult doesn't have as easy a time. He or she has linguistic habits of long practice that impede the total acceptance that learning a new language demands. However, the adult novice can bring to the situation a tool that children don't yet command: analytical reasoning. The adult can look at some examples, formulate a rule, and consciously apply that rule to new situations. The results may be halting speech for a while, but as the adult practices speaking and listens to other talk, fluency increases. People who learn vegetarianism as a "second language" must use the same kind of analysis, experimentation, and practice if they are to become nutritionally "fluent". Their children, however, can then grow up as "native" vegetarians.

Since becoming nutritionally "fluent" is of the same magnitude of importance as learning a second language in order to survive in a foreign country, vegetarian parents need to be reassured that they can raise their children with the same principles on which they live without endangering their children's health. This reassurance can come through talking with other people who have raised healthy vegetarian children, obtaining nutritional information which specifically addresses their needs, and learning from other cultures. The greatest reassurance will be watching our children grow to be healthy adults who can practice vegetarianism with "native" ease.

Chapter  1

Vegetarian Babies
in Other Cultures

*"Nature's methods, perfected over
millions of centuries, are always
purposeful and nearly always right."*

Dr. Jelliffe, under the auspices of
the World Health Organization[1]

Most vegetarian societies exclude meat from their diet for religious and philosophical reasons; some do so out of economic concerns. The majority of Indian Yogic groups, for example, are vegetarian because their members do not want to take the life of another living being. Many Christian orders, sects, and organizations believe that Christ specifically spoke against the eating of flesh. The Seventh Day Adventists are vegetarians for both religious reasons and health concerns. This chapter describes several other cultures which successfully incorporate vegetarianism as a way of life, whether it be on the basis of philosophy or economy, or both.

The Hunza

There are very few societies which have totally meatless diets for purely economic reasons. Animals are raised or hunted in most places, and on the whole, the realization that raising animals for food is more expensive than raising only plant foods has yet to come of age. In fact, there seems to be only one culture that practices total vegetarianism for economic reasons: the Hunza of the Himalayas, who live in an extremely isolated part of the world. The amount of land that is available to them is quite limited, and as a result they have developed a vegetarian culture as the most economical way in which to live.

The Hunza people are some of the most extensively studied vegetarians. They have a reputation for being the healthiest, longest-living people in the world; there is apparently no disease in Hunza, despite a population of 30,000. Their good health is the natural result of clean living conditions, vigorous work, positive attitudes toward life, and sound diet. They have been able to maintain their traditional diet because of their physical isolation from civilization; the country of Hunza is located 7,500 feet above sea level in the Himalayas, surrounded by mountain peaks rising over 20,000 feet. Melting glaciers supply the people in the Hunza valley with mineral-rich water, which they use for drinking, cooking, and irrigation.

Fresh foods are the largest part of the diet. The Hunzas eat seventy percent of their vegetables young and raw; cooked vegetables are prepared with only a small amount of water. The resulting vitamin and mineral-rich water is eaten with the vegetables. Grain is ground daily to perserve freshness. Unlike any other people in the world, the Hunzas regard apricots as a staple in their diet. Both the fruit and the seed are eaten at most meals. Both are also dried. The Hunzas press a fine oil, rich in vitamin E, from the kernel and use it for cooking and as a cosmetic. Since milk is always used the day it is drawn and is only taken from healthy goats who have never been fed chemically "fortified" foods, there is no need for pasteurization procedures. However, milk is stored in the forms of butter, cheese, yoghurt, buttermilk and whey.

Hunza children are breastfed until three years of age, with intentional spacing between children usually practiced by the parents, so that each child can receive all the breast milk available. Because the Hunza diet is an excellent one, good health is passed by the mother to the child, as described by G. T. Wrench in *The Wheel of Health:*

". . .the breast milk of the Hunza woman is as much derived from Hunza food as is the blood of her womb. Her breastfeeding is only a continuation of the period when she is an intervener between her offspring and the Hunza diet. The breast milk itself is a specially manufactured method of conveying that diet to the child."[2]

The adult Hunza diet is gradually introduced to the Hunza baby over the second two years of his or her life. The strength of adult Hunzakuts and the absence of any dental decay or disease suggest that the children are getting the kind of nutrition necessary for their optimal growth and development.

The Macrobiotic Philosophy

The macrobiotic philosophy, which originated in ancient Japan, incorporates vegetarianism for spiritual reasons. It is based on a concept that divides the aspects of the universe into two polarities, yin and yang. Basically, yin is the quiet principle, simplicity, and receptiveness; yang is the moving principle, effortlessness, and creative action. According to this theory, a balance between the two opposites is necessary for optimal spiritual, mental, and physical development. Foods are classified according to the yin and yang they contain, and recipes balance combinations of foods. However, George Ohsawa, the author of *Zen Macrobiotics*, the major work designed to explain macrobiotics to the Western world, stresses again and again that "macrobiotic living is not a rigid adherence to a set of rules."[3] He suggests that parents should study the philosophy of macrobiotics and increase the understanding of themselves before having children. He believes that parents should be aware that children have good intuition about eating and drinking. For example, since a child knows when he or she is thirsty, parents should provide liquids accordingly.

The issue of milk use is important in macrobiotic theory on infant nutrition. In a book called *Milk: A Myth of Civilization*, published by the Ohsawa Macrobiotic Foundation, Dr. Morishita states that it is important for the body to have abundant calcium levels. But he maintains, as do other people, that it is possible to obtain sufficient calcium from vegetable origins rather than from meat products. From birth to about one year of age, the child nurses, gaining sufficient calcium from the mother's milk. After that time, the child eats vegetables. The foods highest in calcium are leafy green vegetables (especially kale, mustard, collards and dandelion greens), sesame seeds, and soy milk. Blackstrap molasses, soybeans, carob and fruits (especially figs, apricots and dates) also supply calcium. The calcium in fruits is particularly absorbable.

There is an important relationship between protein and calcium intake that is best described by Vic Sussman in his book, *The Vegetarian Alternative*, which suggests another reason why plant sources alone can provide sufficient calcium to vegetarians:

"The Food and Nutrition Board has set an RDA (recommended dietary allowance) for calcium but it carries an important qualification for vegetarians: excessive protein intake tends to limit calcium absorption, thus increasing one's daily calcium needs. Most of the world's people don't eat as much protein as do North Americans. The World Health Organization's RDA is 400-500 mg. of calcium daily. But the Food and Nutrition Board, recognizing that U.S. residents habitually overeat protein, has set the RDA at 800 mg. for adults."[4]

He then goes on to say that since vegetarians' protein intake is nearly equal to the RDA of the World Health Organization, they can usually safely eat less calcium, depending, of course, on individual needs.

Emphasizing the ability to get sufficient calcium from plant sources alone, Ohsawa and his followers also believe that it is wrong to drink milk from other animals. They feel that the milk of an animal is intended only for its offspring and is not suitable for feeding to other species.

Even though milk from other animals is unacceptable in the macrobiotic diet, all mothers are encouraged to nurse their children until at least one year of age. If a mother's milk supply is low during this time, she eats a sweet brown rice gruel covered with tahini or ground walnut sauce. The child is given milk made entirely from grains and seeds if it becomes necessary to supplement the mother's lowered milk supply. Ohsawa suggests adding grains and cereals in pureed form to the nursing baby's diet at about six months of age. He recommends that the child not eat vegetables until one year of age. But he also says:

"Bear in mind that the ages at which these foods are added are only approximate. You must be flexible. All depends on your judgment and the constitution of your child."[5]

Other guidelines that Ohsawa gives for the feeding of babies are:

1. Only natural foods should be given, with no preservatives or chemicals used in any stage of growth or preparation.
2. Until the age of six, a child should have very little salt. In the macrobiotic philosophy, salt is seen as a very potent food additive. "Too much salt or the total lack of it produces little activity. If a particular youngster is inactive and listless, if his natural tendency to move has been curtailed, salt should be decreased."[6]

3. When vegetables are introduced, they should be one -third of the total amount of grain in a meal.
4. A child who sucks his or her thumb is indicating a need for iodine and calcium. The way to meet this need is to roast, crush and then sprinkle small amounts of wakame, a Japanese seaweed high in both calcium and iodine, over the child's rice daily.

Finally, Ohsawa says, "Above all, learn from your children. Observe them carefully—they will teach you to have confidence in life . . ."[7]

The Marquesans

The Marquesans live on a South Pacific Island that is described as a Polynesian paradise by Sally Devore and Thelma White in their book *The Appetites of Man*. They are not pure vegetarians, for they eat fish as a main part of their diet. However, I have decided to include them as a vegetarian culture because seafood is the only meat they eat (similar to the diets of many people who feel that they are essentially vegetarians), and because seafood is not included as part of the diet of babies in the Marquesan culture. Instead, local fruits and vegetables are combined to make nutritious baby foods, as is described later in this section.

The Marquesans were discovered by Europeans in the 18th century. The islands lie in the tropic zone, with warm weather all year round. Traditionally the villages have been built near once-volcanic mountains. These sites provide soil that is extremely rich in minerals, raising the nutrient quality of all foods grown there. When the Marquesan Islands were "discovered," the natural good health that the native population had developed quickly faded. The Europeans brought processed foods and diseases, both of which had a devastating effect on the islanders. The population of approximately 120,000 in the late 18th century dropped to only 1,000 by 1920. Ironically, this drastic change also saved the culture; all the foreigners (mostly the French and various missionaries) decided that nothing of use was left on these islands, and abandoned them to the remaining native population. According to Devore and White, the Marquesans were able to take the unusual step of reasserting their original cultural identity and food habits. The island population increased to over 6,000 by 1972, and thanks to their relative isolation, the Marquesans are once again healthy people.

Reclaiming their cultural heritage has wiped out malnutrition. Now children eat no prepared babyfoods and no meat, although seafood is eaten by the adults. Seafood is the only meat eaten by the Marquesans, since game animals are in such small numbers on the islands.

Instead of meat and prepared babyfoods, parents make a preparation for their babies from local fruits and vegetables:

"After a year or so of breastfeeding, the mother supplements the infant diet with a sort of porridge made from the albumen of the immature coconut and starch from grated native arrowroot. A nutritionist who visited the islands analyzed the chemical composition of the coconut through its various stages of development and discovered that the very young nut is low in calories which increase as the coconut matures. They are extremely rich in phosphorus, iron, thiamine, riboflavin, niacin, ascorbic acid, and vitamin E, and when eaten in combination with breadfruit, taro root, or other starchy vegetables, provide the major portion of nutrients needed for good health."[8]

The health of the young Marquesans is a testament to the natural foods diet that these people have chosen as a way of life.

Vegetarian Babies in "Developing" Countries

Malnutrition is a very common problem in many "third world" countries. Often animal populations are low in number, and usually the meat that is available is so high priced as to be unaffordable to most families. Added to these factors is the influx of highly processed foods from industrialized countries which destroys any naturally healthy diet patterns that these peoples might have.

Malnutrition is so common in such countries as Sudan, Nigeria, Jamaica, Syria, India, the Philippines, Malaya, and Indonesia, that several international efforts have been made over the last thirty years to solve this problem. The World Health Organization, the Indian Council of Medical Research, and the Medical Research Council in London are among the groups working against malnutrition. Their basic philosophy is counter to the traditional U.S. assistance approach, and is described by D. B. Jelliffe, a former World Health Organization Visiting Professor of Pediatrics:

"The spread of technological civilization has so far done little to help [malnutrition] and in many cases may have worsened the position by destroying or making impossible old and well-tried beliefs and practices without supplying the means for newer methods."[9]

The solution to malnutrition he suggests is a difficult one for modern technology because of its seeming vagueness or vastness:

"No absolute rules for infant feeding can be laid down and methods must be varied to suit the particular locality... intended improvements must always be based on... local customs and beliefs."[10]

The Indian Council of Medical Research explains further:
"One of the basic and important features of all these recipes is that they are based upon foodstuffs available locally, and also that the food items are traditionally acceptable to the community. They do not contain any processed ingredient or food material which has to be brought from the outside."[11]

After a preliminary assessment of the nutritional status of infants in fourteen subtropic and tropic countries, Jelliffe developed a wide range of recommendations to improve infant feeding practices. Although he encourages the use of animal foods wherever possible, he acknowledges the wide unavailability of animal products in the tropical and subtropical countries, and says, "It is of great importance to make the best possible use of all locally available plant protein foods."[12] He then looks at the various cultures to determine what locally available plant protein foods can best be used. In Egypt, he considers a mixture called *mhallabiah* to be "the most suitable local food for the weanling." *Mhallabiah* is a mixture of cornstarch, ground unpolished rice, ground almonds, milk, sugar and water. In Calcutta, a gruel made of boiled germinated grams (legumes) was considered of greatest nutritional significance, since an increase in the content of ascorbic acid, carotene, niacin, thiamine, riboflavin, and protein is produced by the process of germination. In Lebanon and Syria, *burghul* (a wheat preparation) and *hommos* (a chick pea preparation) are cited as two important foods. In Damascus, the two are mixed together in a ⅔ *burghul* to ⅓ *hommos* proportion. A little sour milk is added to make a smooth, appetizing paste. Another food, *kishkeh*, is made "by adding 3.5 litres of leban (soured milk) to 2.5 kg. of *burghul*. After drying, the final product is reported to keep for at least a year."[13] In Bengal, a combination of various legumes and rice was already being used by adults; a paste could be made to adapt this mixture to the young child. In Turks Island, a dish of boiled, sieved red peas and rice can similarly be used. In Indonesia, a steamed rice and tofu dish was considered to be of high value. Dr. Jelliffe considers legumes to be "undoubtedly the most valuable vegetable food."[14] Chick peas are in turn the best legume; a palatable paste is most easily made from them. Jelliffe reported that chick peas prepared with wheat, bananas, and palm sugar are already being used successfully in infant feedings in the Eastern Mediterranean.

One of the highest priorities in the improvement of infant feeding recommended by Jelliffe is better maternal nutrition, and breastfeeding as the only infant food for the first six months of life and as a major food for as long as possible thereafter. Good maternal nutrition, he argues, will prevent many problems caused by unsanitary food preparation and storage as well as by the lack of money to buy more expensive baby food products. When considering what the best weaning foods are, he comments:

"All over the world, in the temperate zone as well as in the tropics, the first semi-solid foods are almost always starchy gruels and pastes . . . there is no reason to believe that this is not the correct method of initiating this phase of infant feeding although . . . this must be rapidly followed by a much wider range of foods, including particularly plant proteins."[15]

Finally, Jelliffe put considerable emphasis upon working with the various cultures to develop a sense of community spirit and pride within town and village areas in order to effect long-term improvements in infant nutrition.

In 1974, the Working Party of the Indian Council of Medical Research reported on their studies of weaning and supplementary foods in six areas of India. Kwashiorkor, a protein-calorie deficiency disease, was highly prevalent in all areas in young children. They state that "protein-calorie malnutrition is essentially a disease that occurs during the crucial transitional phase of a child's life from breast milk to other types of foods."[16]

In order to combat this problem, the Working Party developed many recipes made almost entirely of plant proteins. The criterion for the recipes was that:

1. they must be preparations capable of easily being cooked at home;
2. they must be able to be made at home in bulk and stored for some time;
3. once in storage they must be easily available to be used as "instant" infant food by mixing with water or milk.

In addition, a high acceptability of the foods by the children was a criterion, because it was felt necessary for the children to consume the foods in amounts which provided 300 calories and 6-8 g. protein in addition to their present diets to combat kwashiorkor. Here are some of the recipes developed by the Working Party of the Indian Council of Medical Research:

1. Khicheri
   75 g. Rice   100 g. Spinach
   50 g. Lentils   10 g. Oil
   (Proteins - 19.3 g.)
   (Calories - 549)

2. Khichuri
   50 g. Rice   60 g. Potato   15 g. Oil
   50 g. Lentils   60 g. Papaya
   (Proteins - 17 g.)
   (Calories - 554)

3. Foxgram porridge
   30 g. Sprouted fox gram flour (local legume)
   10 g. Roasted ground nut flour
   25 g. Ripe plantain (variety of banana)
   (Proteins - 11 g.)
   (Calories - 217)

4. Cholam adai

25 g. Cholam flour	8 g. ground nut oil
20 g. Roasted Bengal gram	4 tsp. water
(chick pea) flour	
18 g. Jaggery (palm sugar)	
5 g. Coconut scrapings	
(Proteins - 7.4 g.)	
(Calories - 325)	

The recipes were tested on two hundred children between the ages of six months and three years. All showed significant growth in weights and heights over a twelve-month period. Also, hemoglobin levels taken from children receiving these recipes showed significant increases. The one problem with the studies is that vitamins A and B complex were not considered in the development of recipes, since the aim was primarily to combat kwashiorkor. Isolating only a part of the nutrient needs of a child is not the best way to produce the healthiest of people, although these recipes do contain some of the necessary vitamins as a by-product of their use.

In the conclusion of this study, the Working Party states: "It is generally agreed that the problem of protein-calorie malnutrition can only be solved by educating rural communities to effectively utilize inexpensive locally available foods . . ."[17]

Although it is not explicitly stated, the indirect message from the research conducted in "developing" countries is that a vegetarian diet is the most economical, practical, and acceptable path to follow in combatting malnutrition. If the children grow up to be healthy adults, no doubt they will confidently offer a vegetarian diet to their children in turn. This is the beginning of a vegetarian tradition that may save many lives.

A Success Story

Vegetarian parents sometimes feel alone in their efforts to raise vegetarian children. A "success story" is quite encouraging. The Farm, a spiritual community based in Tennessee, is an example of a "new" vegetarian culture that is working. (The Farm is also involved in humanizing the birth experience for parents and children and has produced a wonderful book on that subject called *Spiritual Midwifery*.)

Steven Gaskin, the founder of the Farm, describes in his introduction to their "family cookbook" why the members are vegetarians:

"We are vegetarians because one-third of the world is starving and at least half goes to bed hungry every night. If everyone was vegetarian, there would be enough food to go around and no one would be hungry."[18]

The Farm Cookbook describes how a child should be fed. No animal products, including milk and eggs, are used. A vitamin B_{12} supplement is given to the baby who has been weaned, as well as to all adults, since B_{12} is the one vitamin not available in plant foods. Mothers are encouraged to nurse, at least for six to eight months. Strained vegetables, fruits, and processed pablum are introduced to babies after four to six months; starches and unprocessed grains are given after six to eight months. Soy milk, soy yoghurt, and tofu are introduced when the baby is seven to eight months old, but not before, because his or her digestive system is not ready for soy products until that time. *The Farm Cookbook* also mentions that tofu, although very easy to digest, contains very concentrated protein and must be accompanied by lots of liquid for proper usage by the body. Mashed beans and bean soups made from legumes other than soybeans are given to the child a month or so after soy products. Soybeans as such are hard to digest unless they are very well-cooked; some children can't eat them until the age of two or three years.

The people at the Farm feel that protein is the major nutrient to consider in raising a vegetarian child. They suggest that two-thirds of the recommended daily allowance for protein (twenty-four grams per day for children up to three years old) should come from soy products, such as soy milk soy yoghurt, tofu and soybeans. One-third should come from vegetable and grain combinations. Three cups of soy milk or half this amount of soy yoghurt fills the RDA for this age. Vitamin D and B_{12} supplements are recommended. Nutritional yeast is sprinkled on the food of all babies after eight months of age.

Parents at the Farm have community support in their efforts to raise healthy vegetarian children. The Farm exemplifies the growth of a new vegetarian culture based on knowledge of nutrition, cultural borrowing, and group sharing.

An Additional Note of Reassurance

Babies possess an innate sense of what their bodies need; parents need not worry about their children's diet if a variety of foods is made available and if that variety includes all the nutrients needed for full health and growth. Babies *can* choose what their bodies need. Dr. Clara Davis, working at the Children's Memorial Hospital in Chicago during the 1930's, used a diet which attempted to reproduce the diet of "primitive" peoples in her classic experiment on appetite as a guide to children's nutrition. The food list included foods of both animal and vegetable origin. However, Dr. Davis stated that the specific foods used were not important, as long as the list adequately provided all the nutrients needed for growth.

Dr. Davis wanted to determine whether or not babies would choose to eat well-balanced meals when given a choice of natural foods. Her study of fifteen children, reported in the *Canadian Medical Association Journal* in 1939, supported the hypothesis that babies do have an innate judgment which will keep them healthy. The "trick," however, was to offer only unprocessed, natural foods. The babies, ranging from six to eleven months of age, had never been given any foods to supplement their mothers' breast milk. Each child was offered a tray with a wide variety of foods on it at each meal. Each food was in a separate dish. When a baby reached toward a food, the attending adult would then offer a spoonful of that food. At any point, a baby could refuse or choose any food displayed on the tray. No food was offered without a signal from the baby being fed.

The results of this study were impressive. Although babies went on food "binges" and ate quite unorthodox combinations of foods at various meals, each baby, in his or her own way, ate well-balanced meals, according to nutritional standards. The experiment, which lasted for over a year for most of the babies and up to four years for some of them, produced extremely healthy children. Even the children who drank little milk had excellent bone growth, which undermines the popular idea that bone growth depends upon the substantial calcium intake of milk. Two of the children who displayed signs of rickets at the beginning of the study seemed unconsciously to choose high calcium foods such as cod liver oil in greater quantity, and in effect were able to cure themselves by their diet without any interference from the adults.

Dr. Davis was quick to note that self-selection does not produce healthy babies if the foods are poor in quality. She felt that a parent's responsibility is to offer only nutritionally sound, unprocessed foods of a fairly wide variety. She believed that if children are given natural foods and free choice at each meal, the conflict between appetite and nutritional requirements will be resolved. As the editor of a reprinting of her study remarked, "children old enough to feed themselves are wise enough to select a balanced diet when given an adequate variety of wholesome foods from which to choose. Their wisdom comes from the appetite, an exquisite mechanism that is foolproof as long as it isn't baffled, misled, or seduced by refined foods . . ."[19]

Being a vegetarian is more than not eating meat. Finding out about other peoples whose whole lives are based on vegetarian philosophy can be deeply inspiring. Every group of vegetarians has some ideas that will aid in our growth as vegetarian parents. Having a feeling for the universality of vegetarianism, whether as an integral part of a culture or as a solution to the problems of malnutrition, can help new vegetarians to better understand their own philosophies.

Chapter  2

The Healthy Vegetarian Baby

"Judging by numerous references in current nutrition literature, many people believe that life is somehow more difficult for nonmeat eaters. Vegetarians are seen as having to work harder, chew more energetically and generally exert themselves to an unreasonable and unwarranted degree to obtain their protein from the plant world."

Shirley Moore and Mary Byers, as quoted in *The Vegetarian Diet*[1]

"Man evolved for 150 million years on primarily a raw vegetarian diet. . .Man's ancestors provided him with a system that is ideally suited to the digestion of raw fruits, vegetables, nuts and seed—the original diet."

Karen Cross Whyte as quoted in *The Original Diet*[2]

A healthy vegetarian baby comes from healthy, nutritionally aware parents. Because a baby, both before and after birth, is developing more quickly than at any other time of life, he or she has different nutritional needs than an adult. Parents must be aware of these needs and must know how to meet them in order to have a healthy child.

Most meat-eating families can provide the nutrients a baby needs without much nutritional awareness because meat does provide substantial protein, B vitamins, trace minerals and other vitamins to a diet. Unfortunately, animal products also have a number of unwanted, non-nutritional aspects, such as a high level of pesticide residues and synthetic hormones and also a high cost of purchase. I believe that meat-eaters also carry some emotional and spiritual responsibility for the death of living creatures.

Vegetarians avoid the negative aspects of meat-eating and benefit from this freedom by becoming more aware of what and how they eat. After a while, a vegetarian learns what combinations of food yield the most balanced diet, and eating is never again the tiresome process of "meat, potatoes and vegetables" for dinner. Instead, it is the excitement of preparing a tremendous variety of foods—one day you may combine grains and seeds for protein, another day grains and legumes, and still another day legumes and seeds. Once you learn the basic concepts of vegetarian nutrition, the fun begins.

This chapter provides some of the basic information you will need to raise a healthy vegetarian baby. If you are already a vegetarian, many of these facts will be familiar, but remember that being a *vegetarian parent* is slightly different than being a *vegetarian*. The difference is an extension of the responsibility towards another being that any new parent takes on. It is probably better to be unsure of yourself as a vegetarian parent and learn as much as you can about nutrition, than to be overly confident and take unnecessary risks with a growing child.

What Is "Health"?

Health is not easy to measure. The word often refers only to bodily health, to that state in which all bodily systems are functioning efficiently; but even this definition is not always clear cut. Peggy Pipes, in her college textbook, *Nutrition in Infancy and Childhood,* offers the following definition:

"A normal healthy child grows at a genetically predetermined rate that can be compromised or accelerated by undernutrition, imbalanced nutrient intake, or overnutrition. Progress in physical health is one of the criteria used to assess the nutritional status of populations and of individuals."[3]

I find this definition a useful one because it gives a clear picture of some of the problems. For example, how can anyone ever know what the predetermined genetic rate of development is for any one child? The criterion "progress in physical health" has often been interpreted to mean "bigger is better," which unfortunately has led to much childhood obesity. The best definition of health takes into concern each child and all of his or her individual needs. Does the child seem happy? Is she or he gaining weight? How big are the parents? How often does he or she get sick? How much energy does he or she have? A doctor tries to compile all of this information when examining a baby.

A problem can occur if the doctor carries dietary biases into the appointment. If he or she believes that vegetarian babies are less likely to be healthy than meat-eating ones, he or she may worry about the baby's welfare. A worried doctor can foster worry in a parent, and a worried parent may create in his or her child tension about eating. If a doctor thinks all children *should* triple their weight by a certain age, and *should* be eating cereals by the age of three months, or if he or she thinks that *all* babies need iron supplements by the age of four months, then these beliefs will influence the way the doctor sees the child. It is hard to use guidelines as they were intended; sometimes they can become absolute rules.

Good health, then, can only be viewed subjectively, and must be guided by some objective knowledge and some intuition. There is objective information available about what amounts of vitamins, minerals, carbohydrates and proteins on which babies seem to thrive, but even the members of the National Academy of Science, who have developed the RDA charts, stress strongly that:

"Diets are more than combinations of nutrients. . .present knowledge of nutritional needs is incomplete. . .RDA should not be confused with requirements. . .Differences in the nutrient requirements of individuals that derive from differences in their genetic makeup are ordinarily unknown. Therefore, as there is no way of predicting whose needs are high and whose are low, RDA (except for energy) are estimated to exceed the requirements of most individuals and thereby ensure that the needs of nearly all are met."[4]

That statement is not very reassuring if you as a parent want to know *exactly* how much iron or calcium your child needs. But if you understand that the guidelines are only guidelines, and adapt them to your individual child, you should have a healthy baby. Having a doctor regularly check the health of your baby is also helpful, because not everyone can see everything at once. A doctor partial to a vegetarian diet is certainly preferable, but not essential to provide this extra input. Other vegetarian parents can also be helpful in easing specific worries about nutrition that you may have.

Kinds of Healthy Vegetarian Babies

There are two major kinds of vegetarians, those who eat dairy products and those who do not. A third category includes the large group of "partial vegetarians." There are also small vegetarian groups who are vegan extremists.

VEGANS

Vegans eat no animal-based products such as milk, butter, eggs, and lard. This group is not a part of traditional American nutritional culture and scares many doctors and nutritionists. It is the primary target of most research on the health status of vegetarians. The protein, iron, calcium, and B vitamins that meat products supply must be obtained through other means by vegans. There is very little modelling for these alternatives in mainstream American culture.

LACTO-OVA-VEGETARIANS

Lacto refers to milk and milk products, while *ova* refers to eggs and egg products. There are lacto-vegetarians and ova-vegetarians, but most of these people include both eggs and dairy products in their otherwise non-meat diet. The American Academy of Pediatrics, the National Academy of Sciences, and the American Medical Association have all sanctioned the lacto-ova-vegetarian diet, and no longer view it as a fad.

PARTIAL VEGETARIANS

This group is composed of those who occasionally eat meat, usually seafood or chicken, and who also eat dairy products, but who eat vegetable foods as the mainstay of their diet. This is, of course, the least controversial diet and one being increasingly adopted by those meat eaters who are becoming concerned about the pesticide residues and other poisons found in meats. Lower meat intake has been correlated with a lowered cholesterol level and a healthier cardiovascular system, and therefore, with better overall health. The rising cost of meat is often an additional motivator to become a partial vegetarian.

RAW FOODISTS AND FRUITARIANS

Two small vegetarian groups are those people who eat only raw foods and those who eat only nuts, fruits, vegetables, and seeds that have dropped from a plant. These are very risky diets on which to raise babies, because the variety of foods is so limited. Eating raw foods is an important part of other vegetarian diets, however, and recipes based on raw foods can be included in the diets of all children. The following three books contain interesting raw food recipes:

Sprouts for the Love of Every Body, by Viktoras Kulvinakas — Omango D'Press, P.O. Box 255, Wethersfield, CT 06109.

Original Diet, by Karen Cross Whyte — Troubador Press, 385 Fremont, San Francisco, CA 94105.

Healthy Children, Nature's Way, by Ann Wigmore — Hippocrates Health Institute, 25 Exeter Street, Boston, MA 02116.

Studies of Vegetarian Children

There have been several studies of the nutritional status of vegetarian children. However, time and time again, the results of particular studies are generalized to reflect on the health of all vegetarian children, which is a very inaccurate and irresponsible generalization. For example, two recent studies covered by the media were published in the *American Journal of Diseases of Children,* February, 1979. One study was of fifty-two preschool macrobiotic vegetarian children in Boston. The second was a study of the diet of a group of Black Hebrews. The news reports by the Associated Press, and a press release by the American Medical Association, concentrated on the inadequacy of the diets of these two groups: "A strictly vegetarian diet may lead to deformities and even death for infants and children because it provides inadequate nutrition."[5] A news digest report by the magazine, *Vegetarian Times,* comments on this inaccurate conclusion:

"The first article which appeared in the *American Journal of Diseases of Children* described a study of 52 preschool vegetarian children. The author, Dr. Johanna Dwyer from the New England Medical Center, wanted to test her hypothesis that some vegetarian children were likely to get rickets (a disease characterized by demineralization of the bone, due to vitamin D and calcium insufficiencies), especially if their diets were devoid of all animal products. What Dr. Dwyer discovered was that a strict vegetarian (non-dairy) macrobiotic diet, without supplementation, resulted in rickets some of the time. Dr. Dwyer found no cases of rickets among vegetarian children who drank milk. Nor did she find the deficiency present in all strict vegetarian, macrobiotic children.

"The second article in the *Journal* reported 'multiple nutritional deficiencies in infants from a strict vegetarian community.' This article was based on a group of 'Black Hebrews' who apparently ate a very restricted diet which resulted in severe nutritional deficiencies which ultimately caused the death of a child. But a team of dieticians and medical practitioners met with leaders of this group and the deficiencies were corrected — *without the addition of animal foods.* We cite the following: 'Following their initial hospital treatment, the infants received a balanced vegetarian diet that satisfied both recommended dietary allowances and the dietary philosophy of their parents . . . We have not seen new cases of malnutrition from their community since our intervention two years ago.' "[6]

I strongly believe that malnutrition in vegetarian children occurs mainly because the nutritional information necessary for good health is not widely available. If a parent, or even a group of parents, is trying something that is not accepted by the majority culture, their attempt is hindered tremendously. I feel that rather than destroying the confidence of vegetarian parents with scare tactics through the media, researchers should focus upon how parents feed their healthy vegetarian children. Loma Linda University, associated with the Seventh Day Adventists, has been a wonderful example in its extensive research on vegetarian diets. It has also begun some widespread dissemination of this research to nutrition education groups in particular.

Focusing on the positive side of research shows some of the reasons why parents can encourage their children's health by raising them on a primarily vegetarian diet:

1. Childhood obesity is virtually unknown among vegetarian children.
2. Because no meat and often no dairy products are eaten, levels of cholesterol are very low in vegetarian children (and adults), lowering substantially the risk of heart attacks and arteriosclerosis in later life.
3. Gout and cancer of the colon are extremely rare in vegetarians, with much higher rates observed in meat-eaters.[7]

Nutritional Requirements of Vegetarian Babies

Babies have the same basic nutritional requirements whether or not they are vegetarians. The difference lies in how parents meet these requirements, always keeping in mind the individual needs of each child. You will probably be concerned about the amount of various foods your baby eats. If you have only "healthy" food around the house, there is no need to fear that the child will overeat or get too much of one nutrient. It is only when high sugar and empty calorie "junk" foods are available that a baby's intuitive sense of what he or she needs for optimum growth will be off balance.

The Recommended Dietary Allowances, or "RDA's," are based on age groups: from birth to six months, from six months to a year, and from one to three years. Good nutrition and a healthy child are a result of far more than X amount of iron or Y amount of protein. However, quantities of nutrients can be quantified more easily than the amount of respect or love a child gets, and so form the approach of most scientists towards health. The National Academy recommends that beyond providing the individual nutrients, two additional guidelines should be followed:

" . . . to ensure that possibly unrecognized nutritional needs are met, RDA should be provided from as varied a selection of foods as is practicable . . . [and] . . . as food has no nutritional value unless it is eaten, RDA should be provided from a selection of foods that are acceptable and palatable."[8]

As mentioned earlier in this chapter, RDA's are estimated to be larger than the normal requirement in order to meet most people's nutritional needs. So if your child is getting a little bit less than the RDA, do not automatically panic, unless the child often seems listless or sick. Also, a child's nutritional needs do vary from day to day, so that he or she will probably compensate for a minor omission the next day. Learning and applying the general rules of good nutrition is more important than trying to measure every bite your baby eats.

For children under one year of age, the RDA is based upon an analysis of breast milk of mothers with healthy children. Sometimes, the absorption of these nutrients is less efficient in formulas than in breast milk; therefore, the allowance given is for formula-fed babies:

"A breast-fed infant receives about 60 mg. of calcium per kilogram (300 mg/liter of milk) and retains about two-thirds of this. In contrast, an infant fed a standard cows' milk formula containing added carbohydrate (600-700 mg. of calcium per liter) receives about 170 mg. of calcium per kilogram, but retains 25-30 percent.

Although the breast-fed infant has less calcium available, its calcium needs are fully met by breast-feeding. The allowances recommended for the first year of life apply only to infants fed formulas."[9]

The exception to basing all the RDA on breast milk contents occurs when research has shown that children become less healthy when supplemental foods are not added during the first year. Breast milk contains insufficient iron and contains insignificant amounts of vitamin D for the growing baby's needs after four to six months; therefore, these nutrients must be provided in other ways. Supplemental vitamins are the standard answer, but whole grain cereals (for iron) and exposure to sunlight (for vitamin D) are valid alternatives.

It must also be remembered that as solids are introduced into the diet, a mother's breast milk supply will decrease, and so the RDA must be met by a combination of solid food and breast milk. It is also possible that if the mother's diet and health are poor, the breast milk supply may decrease, in which case the child will probably be hungry and "ask" for supplemental foods.

What Nutritionists Worry About

Nutritionists' concern about vegetarianism and babies is certainly well-meant. Vegetarian parents should be reassured, however, that despite their concerns, most nutritionists are willing to accept a vegetarian diet for babies and young children if they think the parents have a good working knowledge of nutrition and if they pay attention to certain areas where there are potential problems. Getting enough protein, calories, calcium, iron, and B vitamins (especially B_{12} in the vegan diet) is the major consideration. The following are some questions vegetarian parents should be able to answer. In case you don't know the answers, they can be found in the following pages of this chapter.

1. How much protein is needed by a baby? Is this different from the protein needed by an adult?
2. What are the best non-animal food combinations which yield the highest usable protein for a baby?
3. How do amino acids and protein relate?
4. What are the best sources for calcium other than dairy products?
5. What minerals and vitamins are essential to effective calcium absorption in the body?
6. When do iron stores normally run out in babies and what are the most iron-rich foods to feed a baby?
7. Is it possible to get enough vitamin B_{12} from non-animal/dairy products to meet a baby's RDA for B_{12}?
8. What is the relationship between folic acid and vitamin B_{12} deficiency symptoms?
9. What are good sources of B complex vitamins in plant foods?

PROTEIN

Protein is the essential building block of all body tissues, including cell walls, muscles, blood, hair, and internal organs such as the heart and brain. It is needed for the formation of hormones, enzymes, and antibodies. Also, protein can serve as a source of heat and energy for the body if carbohydrate and fat intake are not high enough to meet these needs.

Since babies are growing, they need more protein per unit of body weight than do adults, who need it primarily for maintaining their fully developed body. Babies under a year old need three times as much protein per pound of body weight than do adults; children over a year need twice as much. The National Academy of Sciences explains:

"During the first year of life, protein content of the body increases from 11-14.6 percent and body weight increases by approximately 7 kg. The average increase in body protein is about 3.5 grams a day during the first four months and 3.1 grams per day during the next eight months. By four years of age, body protein content reaches the adult value of 18-19 percent.."[10]

Protein is composed of amino acids. There are twenty-two known amino acids that must be brought together in order to make human proteins. Fourteen of these amino acids are produced by the body, but the remaining eight, often called "essential amino acids," must be supplied by the diet. For a baby there are nine essential amino acids because histidine is produced only by the adult body and must be supplied in the infant's diet.

ESSENTIAL AMINO ACIDS

Histidine	Threonine
Isoleucine	Tryptophan
Leucine	Valine
Lysine	

Methionine (Sulfur-containing amino acids)

Phenylalanine (Aromatic amino acids)

If these amino acids are supplied in the proper proportions, the RDA for protein intake for young babies is as follows:

Age:	Grams of protein:
0-6 months	pounds of body weight times 1
6-12 months	pounds of body weight times 0.9
1-3 years	23 grams

The RDA's for the first six months of life were determined from an analysis of the milk of lactating mothers. Thus, as long as a baby is primarily breastfed, there will be no problem obtaining sufficient amounts of protein with the proper amounts and ratios of the essential amino acids. From six months of age on, the RDA was based on an analysis of the milk and solid diets of thriving babies.

Animal foods supply all the essential amino acids in approximately the right proportions. For the vegetarian who eats dairy products there will usually be no problem with high quality protein intake. For vegans and vegetarians who eat no or few dairy products, it is important to look at the protein quality of grains, legumes, nuts and seeds.

Legumes are weak in the amino acids tryptophan and sulfur-containing amino acids (methionine), but are strong in isoleucine and lysine.

Grains, nuts and seeds are generally weak in isoleucine and lysine, but are generally strong in tryptophan and sulfur-containing amino acids (methionine).

If one combines legumes and nuts or seeds, or grains and legumes, proper amino acid balance will result. The resulting complete protein is more useable by the body. *Diet for a Small Planet,* by Frances Moore Lappe, has extensive information on the amounts of each amino acid in various grains, nuts and seeds, and legumes, but the important thing to remember is that in order to get enough usable protein, foods should be combined in one of the following ways:

1. grains with legumes or nuts
2. grains with milk products
3. seeds with legumes or nuts

In addition, the following combinations form complete proteins:

some grains and *some* seeds:
   breads with sesame or other seed spreads
   rice with sesame seeds

some milk products and *some* seeds:
   milk with tahini

some milk products and *some* legumes
   bean soups with milk
   bean mush with milk or yoghurt
   cheese and garbanzo bean spread[11]

Specific recipes taking these principles into account can be found in the recipe section of this book. It is important to eat complementary proteins together at the same meal. If you are giving your child a balanced diet of grains, legumes, vegetables, fruit and milk products (unless you are a vegan, in which case you will need to substitute fortified soybean milk for the vegetarian dairy milk intake), protein intake will not be a problem.

CALCIUM

Calcium is the most plentiful mineral in the human body, and is found primarily in bones and teeth. In combination with magnesium, it helps maintain a healthy heart. It also aids in muscle growth, and assists in muscle contraction and relaxation. It is essential in the diets of young babies, even before birth, since some teeth begin forming around the fourth or fifth month of pregnancy. A deficiency of calcium during this time cannot be reversed; teeth will be weakened, depending upon the amount of deficiency.

Calcium is not absorbed by the body very well. The one exception is the calcium found in human milk. As mentioned in the chapter on nursing, about sixty-six percent of the calcium in human milk is absorbed, but only twenty to thirty percent of the calcium in cows' milk is absorbed. The high content of the major sugar found in human milk, lactose, is responsible for this efficiency. If the body needs more calcium, it simply absorbs more. Vitamins A and D and the minerals magnesium and phosphorus must be present for the body to use calcium properly. A deficiency of calcium can result in bone malformation, muscle cramps and soft teeth.

Milk and other dairy products are the primary source of calcium. Since the vegan does not eat these foods, it is necessary to find other foods that are high in calcium content, to meet the following RDA's:

0-6 months	360 mg per day	(for those
6-12 months	540 mg per day	children not
1-3 years	800 mg per day	being breastfed)

Some plant sources high in calcium are as follows (as adapted from *Laurel's Kitchen*):

2 tablespoons	blackstrap molasses	280 mg
¼ cup	sesame seed meal	270 mg
¼ cup	carob flour	120 mg
1 stalk	broccoli (cooked)	160 mg
1 cup cooked	kale	200 mg
1 cup cooked	mustard greens	180 mg
1 cup cooked	rutabagas	100 mg
1 cup cooked	dandelion greens	150 mg
4 ounce piece	tofu	150 mg
½ cup cooked	soybeans	65 mg

Although obviously the amounts of each food listed are much larger than you would feed to a baby in one day, you can make combinations and varied forms, such as juices and soups, to meet the RDA for the young baby.

IRON

Iron is essential in the production of healthy blood. It works with protein and copper to produce hemoglobin, which carries oxygen from the lungs to the tissues, and myoglobin, which supplies oxygen to the muscle cells.

If the mother has a good iron supply and if a baby is full term, there is no need to supplement a breastmilk diet with iron until after four to six months. If the child is premature or if a mother has a low iron reading during pregnancy, the stores of iron that a baby is born with will be much lower than otherwise. In either case, some additional iron can be given to the baby during the birth process as described below:

"Regardless of the nutritional state of the mother, there is another prophylactic procedure which should be carried out in order to assure the infant has his rightful supply of iron. This procedure consists of allowing the umbilical cord to cease pulsating prior to its severance following delivery. This measure will increase the infant's blood supply by about 100 cc and will thereby add about 45 mg. of iron to the body store. The importance of this procedure can be appreciated when it is realized that this amount of iron is about twice the amount which the average infant retains from his diet during the entire first six months of life . . . this flow can be facilitated by placing the baby below the level of the placenta; while 'stripping' of blood by massaging the umbilical cord may be helpful if circumstances of labor do not allow the 5-15 minutes necessary for the transfer of placental blood."[13]

For premature babies, however, additional iron supplements may be needed.

After six months, the baby's blood mass has increased to the point where iron must be added. At this point iron-rich foods should be introduced. Low iron levels are not caused by a vegetarian diet, but can occur regardless of the type of diet. Current nutritional theory recommends for all ages levels of iron intake that are difficult to meet without an iron supplement. It should be noted, however, that iron supplements are a fairly recent development. Since most people were not anemic prior to this innovation, it is possible that something such as the widespread use of iron pots for cooking (rather than the aluminum and stainless steel ones used most commonly today) may have provided sufficient iron for good health.

The recommended daily allowances for iron are:

0-6 months	10 mg/day
6-12 months	15 mg/day
1-3 years	15 mg/day

Some iron-rich foods are (as adapted from *Laurel's Kitchen*):[14]

1 cup	prune juice	10.5 mg
1 tbsp.	blackstrap molasses	3.2 mg
½ cup	split peas	1.7 mg
4 ounce piece	tofu	2.3 mf
2 tbsp.	pumpkin seeds	2.0 mg
10	dates	2.4 mg
¼ cup dry	millet	3.9 mg
½ cup cooked	garbanzo beans	3.5 mg
½ cup cooked	pinto beans	3.1 mg
½ cup cooked	spinach	2.0 mg
½ cup cooked	lentils	2.1 mg
1 tbsp.	torula yeast	1.5 mg
5 cooked	prunes	1.8 mg

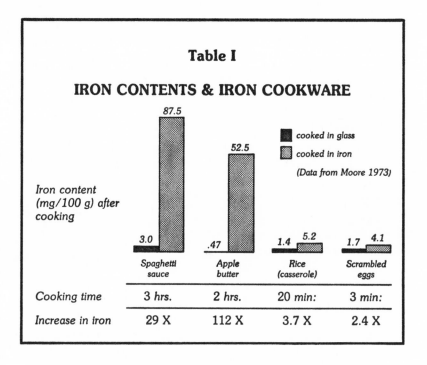

Table I

IRON CONTENTS & IRON COOKWARE

	Spaghetti sauce	Apple butter	Rice (casserole)	Scrambled eggs
Iron content (mg/100 g) after cooking	3.0 / 87.5	.47 / 52.5	1.4 / 5.2	1.7 / 4.1
Cooking time	3 hrs.	2 hrs.	20 min:	3 min:
Increase in iron	29 X	112 X	3.7 X	2.4 X

cooked in glass
cooked in iron
(Data from Moore 1973)

Rice, beet greens, lima beans, chard, kale, almonds, cashews, dried peaches and apricots, egg yolks, and wheat germ also have good iron content (1-2 mg/serving).

The iron content of foods can also be radically increased by cooking with iron skillets and pots. Dr. Jelliffe reports that "stewed apple cut up with an iron kitchen knife and broiled in an enamelled iron saucepan, which was slightly chipped, became as good a source of iron as the best roast beef."[15] *Laurel's Kitchen* provides some further examples, shown in Table I.

Vitamin C is very helpful in aiding iron absorption, since ascorbic acid helps to break down ferric into ferrous iron, which is more efficiently used by the body. The iron content in egg yolks or cereal grains, for example, is high, but is in the form of ferric iron. Drinking orange juice with a breakfast meal is more than just an American traditional breakfast combination; such immediate availability of ascorbic acid is essential to good iron absorption.

B VITAMINS

There are thirteen known B vitamins. They are grouped together because each seems to be essential. to the proper functioning of the other ones. In natural foods, they generally tend all to be present together, so that if a person is getting B vitamins from natural foods, there are not likely to be any deficiencies (except B_{12} — more about that later) among these vitamins.

The B vitamins are essential to the proper functioning of the nervous system, and also help the body to convert carbohydrates into glucose, thus increasing energy availability. These vitamins are necessary for the metabolism of fats and proteins, too. Nutritional yeast is the best natural source of the vitamin B complex. Whole grain cereals are also high in these nutrients. Excessive cooking can destroy many of the B complex. This is one reason the all-American diet tends to be low in B vitamins, while a vegetarian diet, which often includes many raw foods, is less likely to be inadequate. (Goats' milk, by the way, is deficient in folic acid, one of the B vitamins, so a baby fed goats' milk must get folic acid from vegetable foods instead.)

Vitamin B_{12}, however, is the one B vitamin which is not found in any substantial amounts in plant foods. The RDA for B_{12} is small, but must not be ignored:

0-6 months	0.3 mcg./day
6-12 months	0.3 mcg./day
1-3 years	1.0 mcg./day

Table II	
Other Major B Vitamins	**Major Food Sources**
B_1 (Thiamine)	Wheat germ, whole grain breads, cereals, and flours, nutritional yeast, soybean flour, legumes, milk. B_1 is easily destroyed by heat
B_2 (Riboflavin)	Nutritional or brewer's yeast, milk and dairy products, brazil nuts. B_2 is most commonly found in dairy products in most people's diets. Therefore, vegans need to pay special attention to obtaining sufficient amounts of this vitamin. A healthy diet of legumes, green leafy vegetables and whole-grain cereals will usually provide adequate B_2.
B_3 (Niacin)	Nutritional yeast, peanut butter, whole-grain products.
B_6 (Pyridoxine)	Nutritional yeast, egg yolks, blackstrap molasses, wheat germ, bananas, avocados, canteloupe, whole grains.
Biotin	Nutritional yeast, legumes, nuts, cauliflower, sprouts, milk.
Folacin	Green leafy vegetables, oranges, bananas, wheat germ, nutritional yeast.
Choline	No known deficiencies found in humans.

A special note to parents: a tablespoon of nutritional yeast daily supplies the RDA for all B vitamins, including B_{12}. Brewer's yeast and torula yeast do not supply B_{12}, unless they are fortified.

Many vegans also supplement the diet with a B_{12} powder sprinkled on the food, since it is so essential to the health of the nervous system The following are the best non-meat sources for vitatmin B_{12}: There is some evidence that B_{12} can be obtained from sprouted legumes (especially garbanzo), and from the herb *comfrey*, but this is not yet accepted by the standard scientific community as the whole.

1 cup fresh whole milk	1.0 mcg.
½ cup cottage cheese	1.75 mcg.
1 ounce slice cheddar cheese	0.3 mcg.
1 large egg	1.0 mcg.

A severe vitamin B_{12} deficiency will result in damage to the central nervous system. Although there is some indication that *adult* vegans can function without a B_{12} supplement to their diet, it is possible that children cannot grow properly without a B_{12} supplement. Furthermore, another B vitamin, folic acid, which is very available in vegetable foods, can mask a B_{12} deficiency. Shirley Moore and Mary Byers describe the symptoms of a B_{12} deficiency in their book, *The Vegetarian Diet:* "These lesions involve damage to the myelin tissue of the central nervous system, ultimately crippling the victim. Persons with slight damage may complain of tingling sensations in hands and feet. The anemia accompanying these lesions often responds to treatment with folic acid, another B vitamin. Folic acid, however, will provide no help for the nerve damage."[16]

Laurel Robertson and her co-authors (*Laurel's Kitchen*) comment further:

"A deficiency of vitamin B_{12} also results in an anemia which will respond to folacin supplementation, but this only masks the first warning signals of a B_{12} deficiency. For this reason, the amount of folacin that can be legally added to a single vitamin pill has been restricted. . ."[17]

In conclusion, while I do not generally recommend vitamin supplements, I do strongly advise vegan parents to consider a B_{12} supplement for their baby, either through nutritional yeast or a crushed B_{12} vitamin tablet sprinkled on foods daily after the baby is no longer nursing substantially. I refer lactating mothers to the section on B_{12} in breast milk (Chapter Three, pp 80-81).

OTHER VITAMINS AND MINERALS

The following nutrients are essential to growth and proper functioning, and are supplied by most diets, vegetarian or not. Vegetarian children who don't eat empty calorie "junk" foods, however, are less likely to exhibit deficiencies of these nutrients than are children who consume many processed foods.

Vitamins

Vitamin A

Vitamin A helps fight infection and improves tissue and skin texture when taken in proper amounts. It is also needed for good eyesight and night vision, and is used in the synthesis of RNA. There are two kinds of vitamin A from natural sources. Preformed vitamin A is found in animal foods; it can be toxic if too much is taken (over ten times the RDA). Carotene, the other type of vitamin A, is found in vegetables and is not toxic in large amounts. If fruits or vegetables are cooked, mashed or pureed, the carotene in them is more easily absorbed by the body.

RDA:

0-6 months	1400 units
6-12 months	2000 units
1-3 years	2000 units

Foods rich in vitamin A are yellow vegetables and fruits and green leafy vegetables.

carrots	$\frac{1}{6}$ cup cooked	2500 units
sweet potato	$\frac{1}{5}$ large	2550 units
papaya	$\frac{1}{3}$ medium	1765 units

Vitamin C

Vitamin C is necessary for the formation of connective tissue. It helps in healing burns and other wounds, and it fights bacterial infections. It also facilitates the usage of other vitamins by the body.

RDA:

0-6 months	35 mg
6-12 months	35 mg
1-3 years	40 mg

Almost any fresh raw fruit will provide plenty of vitamin C. Vegetables, both cooked and raw, also provide fairly large amounts.

orange juice	$\frac{1}{2}$ cup	60 mg
cantaloupe	$\frac{1}{4}$ melon	45 mg
broccoli	1 stalk (cooked)	160 mg
collard greens	$\frac{1}{4}$ cup (cooked)	35 mg

Cooking and cutting or bruising vegetables destroys vitamin C fairly quickly, because this vitamin is destroyed by contact with the air. To minimize this loss, eat fresh raw fruits and cook vegetables quickly. Vitamin C is destroyed by cooking in copper and iron pans as well. However, since fresh fruit is usually a favorite with babies, there should never be a deficiency. Freshly squeezed orange juice is a good source. There is rarely a toxic reaction to vitamin C, particularly if no vitamin supplements are taken. Vitamin C is used quickly and can't be stored by the body, so it should be a part of each meal.

Vitamin D

Vitamin D is essential for the absorption of calcium, which is why it is often added to cows' milk. The body also needs it to assimilate phosphorus, which is used in teeth and bone formation. In growing children, therefore, a good vitamin D source is important.

RDA:
birth through adulthood   400 IU (international units)

Vitamin D comes either from exposure to the sun or from a vitamin supplement. A little can go a long way, and the body seems to be able to store enough vitamin D during sunny, warm weather to last through the winter if necessary.

If you live in an area that tends towards cloudiness even in warm weather, and your baby does not drink vitamin D fortified milk, it is important to provide a supplement. However, an overdose of vitamin D can be toxic. In the case of a supplement, do *not* exceed the RDA. The RDA assumes little or no exposure to sunlight, so be sure to decrease supplementation during warmer weather if your baby goes outside much.

There is only a trace of vitamin D naturally in breast milk.

Vitamin E

Vitamin E protects many vitamins, particularly A and C, as well as unsaturated fatty acids, from oxidation, which would otherwise render them useless. It is generally a protective and healing nutrient for the body; aging is slowed with a good source of vitamin E, wounds heal more completely, and the muscles of the body function more efficiently.

RDA:

0-6 months	4 IU
6-12 months	5 IU
1-3 years	7 IU

Foods rich in vitamin E are oils, nuts and seeds.

sunflower oil	1 tbsp.	10.3 IU
walnuts	4-7	4.6 IU
wheat germ oil	1 tbsp.	28.3 IU
corn oil	1 tbsp.	3.6 IU

Iron and vitamin E can work against each other, so that if supplements are taken, they should be taken eight to twelve hours apart. Vitamin E is quickly excreted by the body so that overdoses are rare.

Vitamin K

Vitamin K is necessary for production of prothrombin, the active ingredient in blood clotting.

RDA: not established for infants

Foods rich in vitamin K are kelp, leafy green vegetables, yoghurt, egg yolks, blackstrap molasses, polyunsaturated oils.

A vitamin K supplement or yoghurt should be added to the diet if your baby loses blood or if he or she must take antibiotics, which kill the intestinal bacteria that produce this vitamin in the body.

Vitamin P (bioflavinoids)

Vitamin P assists in the effective absorption of vitamin C. Natural sources of vitamin C also contain vitamin P. However, supplements usually do not.

RDA: not established

Minerals

Phosphorus

Phosphorus is found in every cell. In conjunction with vitamin D, phosphorus is necessary for the proper absorption of calcium and some of the B vitamins. It is found in most foods containing protein.

RDA:

0-6 months	240 mg.
6-12 months	400 mg.
1-3 years	800 mg.

Foods rich in phosphorus are whole grains, seeds, nuts and eggs.

cottage cheese	½ cup	185 mg
pinto beans	¼ cup	110 mg.
wheat germ	⅛ cup	165 mg.
pumpkin seeds	2 tbsp.	200 mg.
tofu	4 oz.	150 mg.
garbanzo beans	½ cup cooked	150 mg.
almond meal	¼ cup	140 mg.

Magnesium

Magnesium is needed for many metabolic processes and for proper functioning of nerves and muscles, and is essential to the absorption of calcium, phosphorus, potassium, sodium, the B complex, vitamins C and E.

RDA:

0-6 months	60 mg.
6-12 months	70 mg.
1-3 years	150 mg.

Foods rich in magnesium are fresh green vegetables, soybeans, almonds, oil-rich seeds and nuts, fresh fruits.

prune juice	1 cup	26 mg.
banana	1 medium	39 mg.
orange juice	1 cup	27 mg.
broccoli	1 medium stalk	24 mg.
almonds	15	41 mg.

cashews	14	75 mg.
coconut	¼ cup	14 mg.
peanut butter	1 tbsp.	28 mg.
bread (whole wheat)	1 slice	22 mg.
wheat germ	½ cup	69 mg.

Iodine

Iodine is important in the proper functioning of the thyroid gland, which regulates growth and development.

RDA:

0-6 months	35 micrograms
6-12 months	45 micrograms
1-3 years	60 micrograms

Iodine is found in any plant food grown in an iodine-rich soil. However, since there are some places where soil is depleted, you may want to add a pinch of kelp or other sea water plant to assure a satisfactory amount of iodine in the diet.

Zinc

Zinc aids in the absorption of phosphorus. It is used in the healing process. This is an important trace mineral that is often forgotten in the diet.

RDA:

0-6 months	3 mg.
6-12 months	5 mg.
1-3 years	10 mg.

Foods rich in zinc are wheat germ, nutritional yeast, pumpkin seeds, and foods grown in organically enriched soils.

Table III
TRACE MINERALS

The following minerals do not have an established RDA and are not usually found to be lacking in a vegetarian diet. The information presented below is primarily for interest rather than concern.

Mineral	Function	Foods Rich In
chlorine	regulates acid-base balance and helps maintain connective tissues	seaweed
chromium	used in synthesis of fatty acids, cholesterol and protein; it increases the effectiveness of insulin	whole grain cereal, nutritional yeast
cobalt	functions with vitamin B_{12} in maintaining red blood cells	seaweeds
copper	used in red blood cell formation; it is important in enzymatic functions and vitamin C processes	almonds, leafy green vegetables, legumes
fluorine	helps reduce tooth decay	seaweeds
manganese	important in carbohydrate and fat synthesis and in skeletal development	egg yolks, whole grain cereals, vegetables (depends on soil quality)
potassium	helps control the activity of the heart, the nervous system, and the kidneys	potatoes, bananas
sodium	helps maintain the water balance in the body	almost any plant

A note on sodium: it is very easy to get too much sodium in the diet, since sodium is added to almost all processed foods. Since sodium is found naturally in just about every plant food, adding extra salt (sodium chloride) to the diet is not necessary and can even be harmful, because a high sodium intake can result in hypertension. Giving a baby added sodium in the form of table or even sea salt is not a good idea.

ENERGY

Carbohydrates

Carbohydrates supply energy to the body—energy needs of infants and children are two to three times those of adults per unit of body weight. The body needs B vitamins for proper use of carbohydrates. Refined foods are high in carbohydrates, but usually contain few or no B vitamins.

Suggested Daily Allowance:

0-6 months	115 g
6-12 months	(no figures)
1-3 years	165 g

Foods rich in carbohydrates are: whole grain breads and cereals, fruits and vegetables, nuts and seeds, and beans.

Fats

Fats are the most concentrated form of energy for the body. They produce twice the calories of carbohydrates or protein. They are also important for absorption of vitamins A, D, E, and K.

Suggested Daily Allowance:

0-6 months	28 g
6-12 months	(no figures)
1-3 years	38 g

Foods rich in fats are: vegetable oils, nuts and seeds.

Unsaturated Fatty Acids (sometimes called vitamin F)

Unsaturated fatty acids are important in the process of oxygen exchange. They help regulate blood coagulation and break up cholesterol. Dry hair, dandruff, and skin disorders are some of the effects of a deficiency of this vitamin.

RDA: for infants it is recommended that 3 percent of total caloric intake be from these essential fatty acids.

Foods rich in fatty acids are: vegetable oils (especially soy, corn, sunflower, and wheat germ).[18]

Even though a chapter on health and nutrition must necessarily include specific information on nutrient allowances and the reasons why we need sufficient amounts of each nutrient, I would like to repeat that health is more than the sum of these nutrients. It includes the love that surrounds the child, and the general emotional and intellectual well-being of the child, in addition to the physical health that can be so much more easily measured. Vegetarian parents must remember to include in their baby's diet iron, calcium, protein and vitamin B_{12}, but they should also always remember that diet is just one part of raising a healthy vegetarian baby.

Chapter  3

Vegetarian Parents

"When we change the way we grow our food, we change our food, we change society, we change our values. And so this book is about paying attention to relationships, to causes and effects and it is about being responsible for what one knows. . .we cannot isolate one aspect of life from another."

Wendell Berry, as quoted in
The One-Straw Revolution[1]

Pregnancy and Diet

I have been a "mostly" vegetarian for about ten years—the "mostly" referring to occasional seafood and chicken included in my diet throughout. However, the father of my baby is a much stricter vegetarian; he eats no meat, although he occasionally eats milk and dairy products. While I was pregnant, we mutually decided that we both believed in vegetarianism as a way of life and would raise our child in that way. At the time of the decision, it seemed unreal that I would ever have an actual baby in my arms to whom I would offer a vegetarian diet. My major concern was to make sure I was getting a healthy diet to give the baby a good start. I knew that what I ate was affecting the stores of vitamins and other nutrients that my baby needed to grow and develop inside of me.

I was unaware that my protein needs were increasing as the baby was growing. I had high blood pressure near the end of my pregnancy, although fortunately without any other signs of toxemia (a possible fatal poisoning of the body of unknown causes during pregnancy) accompanying it. The midwife and nurses in a home birth group that I was attending told me that toxemia can sometimes be prevented by a high protein intake, and they advised me to increase my protein intake to 180 grams a day, which was quite a jump, because at that point I was only taking in 60-75 grams of protein a day, on a good day. The Recommended Dietary Allowance for protein for someone of my age group—25-30 years old—during pregnancy is 76 grams per day; Adelle Davis suggests a much higher amount of 90-110 grams per day. I was so full with being pregnant that I could barely eat anything more, much less over 100 grams of additional protein. I tried protein supplements, which tasted awful and killed by appetite altogether, and was generally unsuccessful at raising my protein intake. Fortunately, I did not develop toxemia and gave birth to a healthy son.

I mention my situation because I think it is very important to be aware of nutrition while you are pregnant, and to get into the habit of eating well—ahead of time if possible. Protein needs *do* rise during pregnancy; the answer, however, is not to eat meat, but to start early in pregnancy with higher protein diet. This chapter provides a very complete answer to the question, "Is it safe to be a vegetarian/vegan while I am pregnant?" Taking care of ourselves is the first way we can show love for our babies. Avoiding meats and the chemicals involved in their production, avoiding overly-processed/under-nutritious foods, and avoiding drugs and other non-food chemicals give our babies a much healthier start. Good health for babies begins before birth.

Although a father's role before birth has less effect on the child on the strictly physical level, his support is essential to a mother's well-being, if he is to be involved at all.A father who takes special care to eat well and who helps prepare nutritious, tasty meals during pregnancy is helping to create a healthy baby almost as certainly as the mother who is actually transferring the nutrients to the unborn child. Pregnancy, and nutrition during pregnancy, should be a cooperative venture.

The following article by Pamela Peirce on nutrition and diet during pregnancy is from the Sept./Oct. 1978 issue of a very informative magazine called the *Vegetarian Times*:[2]

Vegetarianism and Pregnancy

Pamela Peirce

If you are wondering whether a vegetarian diet is all right while you are pregnant, the answer is yes. That is, yes, if you take care to meet certain needs.

It probably won't suprise you to hear that there are advantages to a vegetarian diet. Non-vegetarian American women who are pregnant often lack the vitamin folic acid. The symptoms are anemia, lack of energy, and lowered resistance to disease. This vitamin is found in many foods, but it is 50-90% destroyed in cooking. Vegetarians are more likely to eat the raw fruits and vegetables that supply folic acid every day. Many other vitamins and minerals will be more plentiful in a diet rich in natural vegetable foods.

Fiber is one nutrient that is totally lacking in animal-source foods. Fiber is especially important when you are pregnant because food moves more slowly through your digestive tract at this time. The fiber in grains, nuts, beans, fruits and vegetables should help make your pregnancy more comfortable.

A final advantage is that a health conscious vegetarian is less likely to be eating quantities of empty-calorie foods—important because pregnancy is a time when you can afford few empty calories.

Despite these advantages, there are some specific nutrients that a vegetarian who is pregnant must take care to obtain. These are: protein, iron, calcium, vitamin D, vitamin B_2 (riboflavin) and vitamin B_{12}. Following is what you can do to get enough of each.

Protein

You will need more protein while you are pregnant, especially during the last six months. The Food and Nutrition Board of the

National Research Council recommends 30 extra grams a day. While you probably won't count grams, you should become more protein conscious. If you are a lacto-vegetarian, add a couple of servings of low-fat milk products and one or more servings of a complemented protein dish. If you are a vegan, add three or four servings of either soy milk and/or complemented vegetable protein.

Iron

During pregnancy your blood volume increases to meet the needs of the placenta and the growing fetus. More blood means you need to make more iron-containing hemoglobin. In addition, your baby is dependent on you to build up iron stores in its liver that will last for four to six months after birth.

Eggs and milk are relatively poor sources, so all vegetarians need to know plant sources of iron. In general, these sources are beans, peas, nuts, seeds, grains, and vegetables, especially green leafy ones. Sounds like it would be easy to get enough from so many different sources, but each provides only 0.6-3.0 milligrams per serving. You can see that it takes a number of sources to add up to the 18 or more milligrams suggested daily allowance.

In addition, there are substances in some of the above iron sources that interfere with our absorption of iron and other minerals. Oxalic acid, in spinach, New Zealand spinach, beet greens and chard, is such a substance. Instead of these greens, choose kale, collards, dandelion, mustard and turnip greens. Broccoli, cabbage, romaine and loose-leaf lettuce are fair iron sources.

Grains, nuts and beans contain phytic acid, another mineral-binding substance. However, these foods can still be reasonably good iron sources. One reason is that the enzyme phytase has been found in human intestines. Here it digests at least a part of the phytic acid, freeing iron and other minerals to be absorbed.

We can use the minerals in yeast-leavened bread because of the action of phytase in the flour while the dough is rising. Because of this it is wise for vegetarians to include several slices of yeast leavened bread in each day's menu. (If you are making your own bread you can increase phytase action by using a recipe with two risings or by including such acid ingredients as yogurt or fruit juice.)[1]

Another good source of iron is iron cooking pots. If foods, especially acid foods, are cooked in iron pots, they absorb iron which your body can easily use. One-half cup of tomato sauce, baked three hours in a iron pot, increases from 3 to 87 milligrams of iron. Even less acidic foods benefit. In 30 minutes, fried potatoes will change from .45 to 3.8 milligrams, and a rice casserole cooked 20 minutes can increase from 1.4 to 5.2 milligrams.[1]

Calcium

Calcium is important not only for its functions in our bones and teeth, but in blood and other tissues as well. A certain proportion of the calcium in our bones is constantly moving out to be used in other parts of the body. Some is eventually excreted, and the calcium we eat replaces this lost calcium. Calcium is always being excreted, even if we are eating too little to replace it. If we are losing more calcium than we are eating, it is said that we have a "negative calcium balance," and our health and bone strength will suffer.

While you are pregnant, calcium is needed in ever-growing amounts by the developing fetus. Also, stores of calcium are being created in your body to prepare for milk production. Because of these extra needs, the National Research Council recommends 1200 milligrams of calcium, 400 more than for a non-pregnant woman.

This extra requirement is no problem for a lacto-vegetarian. One cup of low-fat milk supplies 352 milligrams of calcium, so four glasses daily will more than meet the allowance. Servings of other low-fat dairy products can take the place of one or more servings of milk.

Vegans should take special care to eat enough calcium. Many of the good vegetable sources of iron are also good sources of calcium. However, the same substances that bind iron, bind calcium. So vegans have a double reason to eat plenty of oxalate and phytate-free vegetables and yeast-raised bread. Soy milk contains only one-fifth the calcium of cow's milk, but you may be able to find a calcium-supplemented soy milk. Or you might choose to take a supplement, like dolomite, which is an inorganic, natural calcium source. You can stir dolomite into soy milk, or into tomato or other thick juice. It's a little gritty, but tasteless, and provides 981 mg. of calcium per level teaspoon.

There is some controversy about how much calcium we need. People in some cultures eat much less calcium than do Americans, and appear to remain in good health. But if you grew up eating a relatively large amount of calcium, your body may have trouble adjusting to less now that you are an adult. A study that was carried out in Norway shows what might happen. Twenty-six Norwegian men were fed a low-calcium diet, than tested for calcium balance. Ten adjusted rapidly, 12 slowly (in nine months to a year), one adapted only slightly and three did not adapt at all.[2]

Vitamin D

Vitamin D helps your body use the calcium you eat much more efficiently. The main food sources are cod liver oil and milk fortified with the vitamin. Another source is the action of sunlight on your skin. Unless you obtain vitamin D from milk or spend a lot of time in the sun, you should take a supplement.

Vitamin B$_1$ (Riboflavin)

Non-vegetarians depend on meat, milk and eggs for most of their supply of riboflavin. There is a little in grains and beans, and this adds up when these become important parts of the diet. However, vegans, especially, should be careful to include some other vegetable sources, such as: all of the greens listed for minerals, and also spinach, almonds, okra, mushrooms,

FOOD GUIDE FOR PREGNANT VEGETARIANS
Eat the number of servings listed for each group daily

Food Group	Group 1 Dairy products and eggs	Group II Legumes, nuts, and seeds	Group III Grain products	Group IV Dark Green vegetables	Group V Fruits and vegetables rich in vitamin C	Group VI Other fruits and vegetables
Lacto-Ovo Vegetarian	4 servings	1 serving of beans and a few nuts or seeds	4 slices of yeast-raised whole grain and 4 other choices	2 servings	1 serving	3 servings of other vegetables and 1-3 of fruit
Vegan	No servings	1 serving of beans and 3 cups of calcium and B₁₂ fortified soy milk,* and 2 small servings of nuts or seeds	6 slices of yeast raised whole grain bread and 5-6 other choices	3 servings	1 serving	3 servings of other vegetables and 1-3 of fruit

Foods to choose from and size of one serving					Choose them yourself
Milk (lowfat, buttermilk, yoghurt) (serving size: 1 cup) Powdered milk (1/4 cup powder) Cheese (cheddar, mozzarella, jack, etc.) (1½ oz.) Cottage cheese (1⅓ cup); Eggs (1 egg) (up to 4 a week)	Beans (soybeans, mung, kidney, black, garbanzo, lima, navy, blackeyed peas, lentils, etc.) (½ cup cooked) Nuts (almonds, peanuts, walnuts, cashews, and nut butters) Seeds (sunflower, sesame, pumpkin, squash, etc.)	Yeasted whole grain breads, rolls, bagels, cornbread (serving size: 1 slice or 1 piece) Hot cereals (rolled oats, cracked wheat, etc.) (½ cup) Cold cereals (shredded wheat, corn, wheat flakes) (¾ cup) Macaroni, noodles, etc. (½ cup) Rice, millet, bulgar, wheatberries, etc. cooked (½ cup)	Collards, • mustard, dandelion asparagus, kale, broccoli, cabbage, dark green lettuce (like romain or butter, *not* head or iceberg lettuce) Serving size: 1 cup raw (¾ cup cooked)	Orange (one) Grapefruit (½), Orange or grapefruit juice (4 oz.) Tomato or pinepple juice (12. oz.) Canteloupe (½) Strawberries (¾ cup) Cabbage (raw) (¾ cup) Green pepper (½) Tomatoes (2)	

Adapted from *Birth and the Family Journal*, Vol. 3, p. 85, with added information from *Laurel's Kitchen*

* or 5 servings of beans and a source of vitamin B_{12} and calcium

avocado, winter squash, squash and pumpkin seeds. Yeast is especially rich in this vitamin.

Vitamin B_{12}

A lacto-ovo vegetarian can probably get all the vitamin B_{12} she needs from milk and eggs, although she might choose a supplement to be safe. A vegan should definitely take a vitamin B_{12} supplement.

Although there are occasional reports that vitamin B_{12} has been found in higher plants, I couldn't track down any reliable research that proves it to be so. B_{12} is produced by bacteria, including the root nodule bacteria of peas and beans. It may also be produced by some algae, although, with the exception of *kombu*, most that seemed to contain it aren't ones that are likely to be in our diet.[3] Vitamin B_{12} is produced in our lower intestine, but so close to its lower end that little if any is absorbed.

The job of analysing plants for vitamin B_{12} is made difficult by the fact that the bacteria which produce it are everywhere. Some water extracts of soil contain as much vitamin B_{12} as milk. Well water, pond water and even the sea, contain significant amounts.[4] One study found vitamin B_{12} in one sample of turnip greens, but later samples were all negative, suggesting that there were bacteria in the first sample.[5]

Nerve damage and anemia from vitamin B_{12} deficiencies develop slowly. One reason is that vegans may be getting some vitamin B_{12} from bacterial contamination of food or water. A second reason is that when little of the vitamin is eaten, our bodies can rescue some "used" vitamin B_{12} before it is excreted and recycle it.[6] A third reason is that a person who once ate animal products will have a three to five year supply of vitamin B_{12} stored in her liver.

However, a woman's stores of vitamin B_{12} are used up much more rapidly if she is pregnant. The vitamin is needed when DNA is created, and DNA must double in each cell nucleus before the cell can divide. Because of this, vitamin B_{12} is of critical importance to the growing fetus.

Vitamin B_{12} supplements do not violate a vegetarian diet. They are made from a bacterial source, and bacteria are a life form that preceeds the plant-animal division.

Supplements

Many women, vegetarian or not, will feel more secure taking a multi-vitamin and mineral supplement while pregnant. While it is no substitute for a good diet, it can cushion the effects of occasional missed or unbalanced meals.

Final Words

Follow all the general precautions for pregnancy: be well nourished before you get pregnant; get special nutritional counselling if you are a growing teen-ager; don't diet or fast while you are pregnant; avoid drugs, coffee and alcohol; get enough rest and exercise sensibly; and don't let a doctor put you on a salt-free diet or on "water pills." The best insurance you have against dangerous toxemia and other problems of pregnancy is a fully adequate whole food diet—vegetarian? Of course!

References

1. Robertson, Laurel, Flinders, Carol, Godfrey, Bronwen, Laurel's Kitchen: A Handbook of Vegetarian Cookery and Nutrition, Nilgiri Press, Berkeley, CA, 1976.
2. Davidson, Passnore, Brock and Truswell, Human Nutrition and Dietetics, Churchill, Livingstone and Edinburgh, London and New York, 1975.
3. Erickson, L. E. and Banhidi, Z.G., "Bacterial Growth Factor Related to B_{12} and Folinic Acid in Some Brown and Red Seaweed," Acta Chemica Scandinavia, 7:167, 1953.
4. Smith, E. L., Vitamin B_{12}, John Wiley, 1960.
5. Evans, H. J. and Kliewer, M., "Vitamin B_{12} compounds in Relation to the Requirements of Cobalt for Higher Plants and

Nitrogen-fixing Organisms, New York Academy of Science Annals, Vol. 112:2, 1964.

6. Herbert, V., "Nutritional Requirements for Vitamin B_{12} and Folic Acid," *America Journal of Clinical Nutrition, 21: 743-52, 1968.*

(Reprinted with permission of Pamela Peirce.)

Lactation and Diet

For the first months of a baby's life, a healthy mother's milk provides all the nutrition that he or she needs. The special care that a mother has been giving herself during pregnancy does not stop after birth, but some of the requirements change slightly. According to the Recommended Dietary Allowances (see Table IV), protein needs drop slightly during lactation. On the other hand, vitamin A requirements rise, as do caloric, vitamin C, niacin, riboflavin, iodine and zinc requirements. Folic acid requirements drop. Notice that requirements for almost all nutrients remain higher than for the non-pregnant, non-lactating woman.

A note on vitamin B_{12} for lactating mothers: In August of 1978, the *New England Journal of Medicine* published two articles which said that vegetarians who eat no animal products (vegans, who do not eat any milk or dairy products) may not have enough vitamin B_{12}, essential to a baby's healthy development in their breast milk. This deficiency should be something for vegan mothers to be aware of in their diets. *Vegetarian Times,* in its Sept./Oct. 1978 issue, reported that adults seem to need less B_{12} than infants; therefore remember that you need to take in extra for your baby during this time. A vitamin B_{12} supplement to the mother's diet during lactation seems to be the most practical answer until more is understood about this vitamin. The members of some vegan communities, such as The Farm in Tennessee, automatically include B_{12} supplements in their diets, and in the diets of their children as soon as the children begin to eat solid foods.

There have been some scares about the pesticide content of nursing mothers' milk, but apparently the statistics are not as bad for vegetarian moms: In an analyisis of the breast milk of meat-eating mothers in the early 1970's a test of 1400 women in forty-six states showed up to ten times the acceptable amount of PCB, two times the acceptable amount of DDT and nine times the acceptable amount of dieldrin. Sussman, in his book *The Vegetarian Alternative*, reports that in 1976,

"The Environmental Defense Fund asked the Environmental Protection Agency to conduct a similar breast analysis of vegetarian women to determine if dietary patterns influenced the accumulation of pesticides in fatty tisues. The results of this second test showed that women on a vegetarian diet had levels of pesticides in their milk two to three times lower than women eating a standard diet."[4]

While this situation is not ideal, if parents grow their own vegetable foods and/or are able to obtain them from organic sources, this level will be even lower.

I was very lucky in that I had no problems with breastfeeding my child: no engorgement, lack of milk supply, or infections. Some mothers may not be so fortunate, but there is a tremendous amount of information and support available to these women or to any mothers who have questions about breastfeeding. I particularly recommend the following books:

Table IV

NUTRIENT REQUIREMENTS
FOR PREGNANT AND LACTATING MOTHERS

	Women age 23-50 (av. 128 lbs.)	Pregnancy	Lactation
Calories	2000	2300	2500
Carbohydrates (g)	300	*	*
Fats (g)	66	*	*
Proteins (g)	46	76	66
Calcium (mg)	800	1200	1200
Iodine (mcg)	100	125	150
Iron (mg)	18	18+	18
Magnesium (mg)	300	450	450
Phosphorus (mg)	800	1200	1200
Potassium (mg)	1950-5850	1950-5850	1950-5850
Sodium (mg)	2300-6900	2300-6900	2300-6900
Vitamin A (IU)	4000	5000	6000
Thiamine (B_1) (mg)	1.0	1.3	.3
Riboflavin (B_2) (mg)	1.2	1.3	.5
Pyridoxine (B_3) (mg)	2.0	*	2.5
Cyanocobalamin (B_{12}) (mcg)	3.0	4.0	4.0
Biotin (mcg)	150-300	150-300	150-300
Choline (mg)	500-900	500-900	500-900
Folic Acid (mg)	0.4	0.8	0.5
Inositol (mg)	1000	1000	1000
Niacin (mg)	13	15	19
Pantothenic Acid (mg)	5-10	5-10	5-10
Vitamin C (mg)	45	60	80
Vitamin D (IU)	400	400	400
Vitamin E (IU)	12	15	15
Vitamin K (mcg)	300-500	300-500	300-500

*information is not available
(from Nutrition Almanac, p. 247)

1. *Preparation for Breast Feeding,* by Donna and Rodger Ewy (Doubleday, 1975)
2. *The Complete Book of Breastfeeding,* by Sally Olds, and Mrvin Eiger (Workman Publishing, 1976)
3. *Nursing Your Baby,* by Karen Pryor (Harper and Row, 1973)
4. *Womanly Art of Breastfeeding,* by Mary Carson (La Leche League International, 1963)

Also, La Leche League has support groups in almost every part of this country which can offer more specific and personal advice than I ever could fit into this book. (Ask your doctor how to get in touch with the local branch of La Leche in your town.) The guidelines that I used concerned quality and quantity of milk: drink lots of liquid (you may notice you get very thirsty whenever you nurse—listen to your body!) and maintain a healthy diet. Exercise and relaxation are also tremendously helpful. In her book, *Let's Have Healthy Children* (now being revised), Adelle Davis offers many formulas and suggestions for increasing both the quality and the quantity of milk.

So read, eat well, love yourself and enjoy your baby. Talk to other mothers, vegetarian and not, for special tips and personal experiences.

Weaning

When my son was eight and a half months old, I developed an infection which was serious enough to require a very heavy dose of Flagyl, a drug which contaminates breast milk and is not good for the baby. I was forced to abruptly stop nursing for two weeks, which gave me a much more sympathetic understanding of mothers who are unable to nurse. It was probably more traumatic for me than for my baby, though; he took to a bottle of goats' milk and yoghurt (mixed and strained to remove the lumps) very willingly, although he was certainly confused by the change. I expressed milk during the two weeks and then started nursing him again. I decided, however, to partially continue the bottle, because it meant my husband had more of a chance to feed our baby, which was an important sharing experience.

Whether weaning means the introduction of a bottle and/or solid foods or the end of nursing altogether, a change from an all-milk diet is a very important time for both parent and child. Suddenly the ease of knowing that all the nutrients are supplied in the correct amounts is gone and must be replaced by a conscious decision about what to feed the baby instead to make sure he or she continues to be healthy. For the vegetarian parent, weaning is often an exciting moment of beginning to share an important world view exemplified by one's diet.

The Vegetarian Working Parent

When my baby was one month old, I returned to work on a part-time basis. I worked three evenings a week while my husband took care of the baby. Although it was new and hard for him, I think my absence gave him a special early relationship with our baby that many men do not have a chance to experience. I was able to express several ounces of milk for each evening I was away. If this ran out, my husband fed him a yoghurt and water mixture. Our pediatrician reassured us that yoghurt milk was easy to digest as well as nutritious. Yoghurt, which contains lactobacillus, an important intestinal bacteria which aids in digestion, is a very good substitute for human milk, especially on such a limited basis.

When my baby was five months old, I started to work during the day so that it was no longer possible to leave him with his father. Fortunately, I was able to find a very good situation in which the caregivers appreciated and accepted my vegetarian feeding ideas as they applied to my son, who was beginning to eat foods.

However, working more hours (five mornings a week) cut severely into my free time and I found that it was difficult to spend a great deal of time making meals for my son. I developed the casserole idea, and the fine grinding of grains which in effect produced "instant meals," both of which are described in detail later in this book. I didn't freeze foods, finding it quicker, or at least as quick, to prepare small amounts from fresh foods than to thaw out frozen portions. I developed a pattern of feeding my son first and then giving him foods he could pick up with his fingers as we ate, so that we could share our mealtimes without requiring that my food get cold as I fed him. I have found in general that feeding a baby is a painless and an exciting activity, despite the time pressure my job added to my daily life as a mother. (Fortunately my husband and I have always shared the making of meals, so that even though he worked all day outside the house while I only worked half a day, we took turns getting our meals ready rather than my having to have a meal on the table when he got home from work.) I have found that although I am not an avid cook, I have really enjoyed preparing foods for my baby. He is willing to try anything once, as the saying goes.

Even though working can add pressure to a family's life, it is possible to make mealtime a relaxed, sharing, and enjoyable time. I never eat frozen prepared foods, and the short cuts I take do not cut nutritional corners, but only time.

Being a working parent should not have to mean that non-working time becomes rushed with a young child. It is possible to remain calm and healthy while being a working vegetarian parent.

Interviews with Vegetarian Parents

It is hard for one person to write a book that will answer all of the questions that anyone would ask about raising a vegetarian baby. I have tried to include what I see as the essential information, as well as some interesting sidelights, and to include references where I do not have the background or space to deal with a subject completely. I decided to broaden the scope of this book by including interviews with vegetarian parents—their insights, experiences and questions. Each of them has a somewhat different life-style than I, and adds her own ideas about raising children as vegetarians. The first transcript is from my own journal, an "interview" with myself, and traces my son's development through a nine-month period of his life.

Five months: I feel very ambivalent about starting solid foods with Nikolas. On the one hand I am excited to be able to try out all the recipes I can think of and to watch his delighted (or not so delighted) expressions as I give him the very little tastes of what I am eating. However, I am nervous about changing from a complete nursing-milk diet in which I *know* he is getting all the vitamins, minerals and proteins he needs. How can I be sure he is getting everything he needs without consulting a food composition chart as I cook each food?

Six months: I am still relying greatly on nursing for Nikolas to get the nutrients he needs. I am mostly introducing foods now to see what he thinks of the taste. He seems to like everything I give him and goes "eh-eh-eh" for more. Sometimes he tries to hold the spoon after he has eaten a little from it. The rest somehow ends up on the back of his head. So far he has tasted yoghurt, apple juice, orange juice, prune juice, nectarines, oatmeal, rice, bananas, peaches, and avocados.

Seven months: It's hard to make sure he gets enough vegetables in his diet—especially the stronger tasting ones like broccoli. I still worry that he's not getting enough of everything and feel relieved only because he is still nursing. The pediatrician says not to worry about the amount of iron he's getting, although everything I read seems to say that a baby's iron stores run out between four to six months. I try to combine orange juice and eggs (the vitamin C in the orange juice assists iron absorption from the eggs) to make sure, though. I tried giving Nikolas some of the packaged iron-fortified baby cereal—he grimaced and spit it out. I tried it and it tasted like gummy cardboard—no wonder! Usually I really like everything I make for him, although I tend to want to salt it for myself. I'm using kelp instead of salt for Nikolas to make sure that he is getting enough iodine.

Seven and one-half months: a typical day's menu:
   Breakfast—cereal with banana and yoghurt
   Snack—apple juice
   Lunch—cottage cheese and applesauce with ground up
      wheat germ
   Snack—nursing
   Dinner—grain and vegetable with yoghurt; juice to drink
      (or egg and vegetable or tofu and grain and vegetable)

Bedtime—nursing
All night and first thing in the morning—nursing

Eight months: Foods that he has tried so far (I haven't been as careful about allergies as the books say to, partly because I figure I started feeding him pretty late, so that allergies are less likely to happen): yoghurt, cottage cheese, banana, apple, pears, mango, papaya, avocado, peaches, figs, prune juic, orange juice, carrots, yellow squash, zucchini, green beans, peas, corn, lima beans, rice (brown rice), millet, barley, oatmeal, tofu, egg yolk, wheat germ, coconut (juice and meat), lentils.

Eight and one-half months: 1 have to stop nursing because of medication that I have to take. How will he survive without the "perfect" diet?

Nine months: Nikolas seems to eat really well when there are other children around—partly he is so entranced by watching them that I'm not sure he is aware that he is eating.

Ten months: I'm back to nursing but my milk supply seems low—I rarely hear him swallow a lot. He wants to eat by himself these days—he bats away a spoon most of the time but will feed himself dozens of peas and pieces of cheese, crackers and lentils. Lentils, in fact, are really a favorite, especially my casserole which has wheat germ, lentils, garlic, onions and egg in it. He loves scrambled eggs made with milk, but spits them out when they are made without milk. He has the most incredible expressions of distaste and even pretends to gag when he doesn't want to eat something—I say "pretends" because sometimes he gags before the food even gets to his mouth and he always smiles or laughs after he gags, in a very knowing way.

Ten and one-half months: He doesn't seem to be eating much of anything, but seems to want to nurse, nurse, nurse, about 85 times a day. He won't eat chunks of food that he used to love; won't eat from a spoon (more than a couple of bites), won't drink more than a couple of ounces from a bottle. He doesn't seem to get frustrated that there is little milk in my breasts, but will suck endlessly. I've been trying different techniques to get him to eat other than nursing. One of the most effective is feeding him in the bathtub while he plays in the water; he'll eat tremendous amounts while he's doing something else. From what I've heard and read this is a common stage and that it is better to have the child enjoy eating even if it means playing at the same time than to force him and set up a bad feeling about food. Nikolas just seems to dislike a formal mealtime, no matter how much fun I try to make it.

Eleven and one-half months: Nikolas has started enjoying mealtimes again and can eat tremendous amounts—practically twice as much as he did a month ago. He doesn't seem to want to feed himself with a spoon although he likes to drink from a cup holding it himself. I try to give him something that he can pick up with his fingers and eat at each meal, because he seems to enjoy that. I usually feed him first and then give him bits and pieces of whatever I'm eating when I eat. He doesn't like peas now—if I give him a spoonful of mushed grains or yoghurt with a whole pea, he will eat the food and casually spit out the pea when he's done—it must take a lot of control not to mash it up as he moves his mouth around the other food! Although I am still nursing, Nikolas drinks 6-8 ounces of milk from a bottle during the afternoon and before his bedtime. The nursing seems to have a last relaxing effect so that he can conk out at night. I've added broccoli and cabbage to his regular vegetables, in combinations with grains, and he likes them fine. He still goes through periods of not eating well during one meal, but then eating well the next one. He definitely lets me know when he is through eating: he shakes his head and pushes my hands away—no question about overstuffing him or forcing him to eat. He doen't seem to like breads and crackers as much as he used to, but loves cheese. When he eats yoghurt, he looks like a TV commercial for a yoghurt company—eating with such eagerness and perfect form. A non-parent friend of mine has asked me if I have to think about what I'm going to feed him next, sounding like it was a burden. I *do* have to think, but I feel like I'm able to create the most wonderful gourmet dishes for my special baby.

One year: Nikolas is learning to share. He gives me his food to eat and wants to eat mine. I like it better, though, when he shares his orange juice popsicle than when he tries to share his baby mush. It's a nice thought, though!

Fourteen months: Nikolas is feeding himself very well these days, so I give him a thick mush food as a main meal most of the time. He uses a spoon, although he turns it over right before it gets to his mouth, so that if the meal is too runny he loses half of it. He can hold a cup alone although he still tends to spill it when he is distracted by anything. He signals to me when he is through eating by dropping his spoon and bowl over the edge of the table, unless I am quick enough to catch it first.

INTERVIEWS

Two people whom I know agreed to fill out questionnaires to share their experiences as first time vegetarian mothers. The following comments come from Barbara Berger, who has a six-month-old baby girl. She has been a vegetarian for about ten years. She doesn't eat meat, fish, sugar or anything with artificial ingredients. Naturally, her daughter has always been a vegetarian, since she is only six months old.

Q. How do your parents feel about your raising your child as a vegetarian?

Barbara: My mother and father find me so different than they are that we reached the point years ago where they don't even comment on things that I do. I imagine, though, that they would feel O.K. about it since they see I'm so healthy on a vegetarian diet myself.

Q. Do you have any hesitations about raising your child as a vegetarian?

Barbara: No, not at all.

Q. Do you feel that you have enough nutritional information for raising a vegetarian baby?

Barbara: Yes—I just use my diet for her, concentrating on foods with iron, since breast milk is lacking in this (*author's note: breast milk is not lacking in iron. Rather, as the child grows older, he or she needs greater iron supplies than is available in the milk. At this point, around four to six months, iron supplementation, through tablet form or through natural foods high in iron becomes necessary—see chapter two.*) Also, I give her Schiff natural vitamins—liquid C and A and D.

Q. How does your pediatrician feel about the issue of raising a vegetarian baby?

Barbara: I never asked, because doctors, even pediatricians, generally aren't knowledgeable about nutrition.

Q. How do you feel about your child eating meat?

Barbara: Probably she will taste it when she is older, and I feel O.K about that. We won't have meat at home, though.

Q. Are there any special foods that your baby eats?

Barbara: One especially healthy food that I give her that she likes is a mixture of yoghurt, molasses (blackstrap) and nutritional yeast. I make unyeasted bread sticks for her to use as teething biscuits. She likes stewed fruit, and especially apricots, which is good since they are very iron-rich. I also feed her squash, yams, wheat cereal, and oatmeal. Sometimes I give her our food ground up through a baby food grinder if it seems digestible enough for her.

Q. What kind of questions do you have as a vegetarian parent?

Barbara: I would like to see the U.S. Recommended Dietary Allowance charts for infants. I would like to know what some good dairy substitutes are that are not as strong as beans. I would also like to know at what ages babies can digest foods like nuts, peanut butter, tahini, and foods sauteed in oil.

Krys Cail has an eleven-month-old son and has been a vegetarian for about ten years also. She avoids meat, including chicken, white sugar, all refined foods, and excess fat and salt. She does eat fish occasionally, but not more than once a month or so.

Q. How do your parents feel about your raising your child as a vegetarian?

Krys: Great! He's huge and healthy. At some point he will need to have a chance to experiment with different kinds of diets and they will doubtlessly help provide that. But his obvious excellent health has helped them finally accept *my* vegetarianism.

Q. Do you have any hesitations about raising your child as a vegetarian?

Krys: Yes, I do. The social stigma of eating "weird" foods seems like it could be a potential problem.

Q. Do you feel that you have enough nutritional information to raise a vegetarian baby?

Krys: I wish more was available. Right now, I go by what I know of adult nutrition, which seems to be adequate, but I would like to know more about babies in particular.

Q. How does your pediatrician feel about this issue?

Krys: I don't know. At the clinic I take my son to, they are too busy running a health care factory to even ask what I'm feeding him. As it is, they think he's a very healthy strong baby but have no idea why.

Q. How do you feel about your child eating meat?

Krys: I figure he should be encouraged to avoid it, but not prohibited. He was offered a hot dog (my idea of the worst possible meat) at a neighbor's picnic. I just watched him. He played with it for five minutes, but didn't seem to recognize it as food, even though the little girl next to him was eating one. He was about nine months old at the time.

Q. Are there any special foods or recipes that your child likes?

Krys: At eleven months, the things he seems to like best are a combination of bulghur, goats' milk, and molasses with some brewer's yeast added. He also likes yoghurt mixed with tahini, and bread crumbs soaked in carrot juice. I found that whole wheat bread crumbs made with a blender or grater easily took the place of the common "baby cereals" at less cost and more nutrition. It's just as convenient, too.

Q. What kind of nutrition questions do you want answered?

Krys: I would like to know more about the protein and vitamin requirements at different ages and weights, what foods contain these nutrients, and what proportions provide the best balance for good health in a baby.

Q. Do you have any other comments?

Krys: Yes! Moss, my babe, was nine pounds six ounces at birth, is close to thirty pounds now at eleven months, and is a real muscle man.

Shelley MacDonald is a macrobiotic mother with three children, aged ten months, four years, and six and a half years. She teaches courses on macrobiotics on the East

Coast through the East-West Institute. Her husband, Tom, is also a vegetarian, and they are raising their children according to the macrobiotic philosophy. The following are excerpts from an interview with her.

Q. How long have you been vegetarian?
Shelley: Although neither my husband nor I were raised as vegetarians, we have avoided meat eating on the whole for almost ten years now. If it's a special occasion like Christmas and someone puts egg in a food, then we will eat it, but we usually avoid dairy products. My husband eats fish once in a while, mostly in the winter.

Q. Why did you become vegetarians?
Shelley: We started out being interested in natural foods and vegetarianism for sheer economic reasons, but it quickly became more than that. We stumbled on to information about macrobiotics which really excited us and decided to follow it up. We also met several people who impressed us with their health and vitality and who turned out to be macrobiotic, which impressed us further.

Q. What is your understanding of the macrobiotic philosophy?
Shelley: First I should say that macrobiotics means eating whole foods, in season, and locally grown as much as possible. We grow most of our vegetables and we intend to grow more grains and beans in the future. We do buy some imported foods, like miso and tamari, but our goal is to make our own. The things we eat from other places we try to obtain from the same latitude zone so that there is some kind of similarity. In macrobiotics, you don't have to adhere to strict guidelines. What and how you eat depends more on you as an individual. There are guidelines, but you may have to step outside of them to achieve a balanced condition in your own body. The macrobiotic philosophy allows and

in fact encourages paying attention to individual needs and strengths and weaknesses. Macrobiotics is based upon a theory of yin-yang. All foods are classified as either yin or yang, and to be healthy your body must have a balance of these two principles. If you are sick, it is usually because you are eating too much of one kind of food, so that the yin-yang balance gets upset. When your body has an overload or an excess of either yin or yang foods, then it has to discharge this extra, which comes out as some kind of sickness. Some foods, such as sugar, are extremely yin and will easily throw you off balance. In fact, avoiding sugar will reduce the severity of any illness. Cereals and grains, especially brown rice, have a good balance of yin and yang within them and so are the staple of the macrobiotic diet.

Q. How do your parents feel about your raising your children as macrobiotic vegetarians?

Shelley: When we were first macrobiotic eaters, it was difficult, because we weren't in very good shape to start out with and we didn't understand the philosophy well enough to know what to do. We both underwent a weight loss, which was hard on our families because they thought we were starving ourselves. In fact, we were eating a lot, but our bodies had some trouble getting used to it — we may have jumped in too quickly. We didn't feel weak, though, even though we were losing weight. That period stabilized and we began to put on weight again and became very healthy. After seeing this change, our parents got over their fears. Now my mother is pretty open to macrobiotics and she says that as long as we are healthy she doesn't care what we eat. Tom's family isn't very interested in food, so when we go to their home, we don't discuss food, but just stay away from meat and sugar until we get home. I guess my parents feel that as long as our kids are healthy, it doesn't matter how they eat.

Q. Do you feel that cooking and eating macrobiotically takes up a lot of time?

Shelley: Our family is structured so that I am home most of the time. I do most of the cooking, except on rare occasions, and a lot of my time is spent cooking. I probably cook two and a half to three hours a day. That's a lot of time, but since I don't work outside of the house right now, I can put in that kind of time. I do know people who hold full-time jobs and still manage to cook macrobiotically for themselves. You just have to plan ahead and store things in the refrigerator. You can eat very elaborately or you can eat simply or you can eat somewhere in between.

Q. Do you have any hesitations about raising your children as macrobiotic vegetarians?

Shelley: My hesitations were more about becoming a parent for the first time. I was totally convinced the diet would work, although I knew I would be facing problems that I hadn't faced with myself. We had more experience with macrobiotics than we had with kids. Now, I feel very sure about it.

Q. How do you feel about your children eating meat?

Shelley: My kids seem to have definite food tastes already established. For example, we were at a folk festival and a man gave my son a hamburger. He took one bite of it and spit it out without anyone saying anything about it to him. We are more concerned with their wanting sugar than meat, because we feel sugar is nutritionally a terrible thing. When Erin went to kindergarten, she went through a period where she wanted to be like the other kids, eating candy and chewing gum. We told her that we function as a family and eat in a very special way and that she had to join in as part of the family. I think that it was more of a social phase for her than a nutritional need or desire.

Q. What kinds of foods did you first introduce to your children?

Shelley: I breast-fed my oldest daughter until she was fourteen months old, my son until he was eleven months, and my ten-month-old is still nursing. I know children who have naturally weaned themselves, but my kids didn't, although they began to show signs that they needed it for attention rather than for nourishment. With my first child, I felt it was important not to give her any solid food when she was very young because her digestive system would be immature. I held off until she was five or six months old. My son seemed interested in solid food when he was around four months old and I felt freer to give it to him because he was my second child and I was less uptight. With my baby I'm just going to wait until he seems unsatisfied with my milk and then give him food.

Being macrobiotic, our diet is based pretty much on whole grains and vegetables. When I introduced food to my kids, it was pretty much cereal that I made myself from brown rice. Sometimes I would add crushed seeds or a little bit of beans. Usually I ground the cereal, but sometimes I would chew the baby's food myself. Then I would put it on the spoon and feed it to the baby. I did that to get the enzymes in my saliva to start digesting the food to make it more digestible for a baby. This is not just a macrobiotic thing — my grandmother from Czechoslovakia did this for her children. I let them chew on a carrot stick or a piece of seaweed and gnaw on bread when they began teething. We adjust our diet seasonally, eating more fresh vegetables in the spring, summer and fall and more grains and beans in the winter. When Luke, my son, started eating solid food, it was summer so I gave him a lot of vegetables. There were some he wouldn't eat. My oldest daughter, Erin, started eating in the winter, so I gave her more grains and fewer vegetables. Both of them have showed definite preferences that are different from the other. Both of them have liked rice from the beginning. Sometimes they have shocked us by refusing dessert-type preparations and just eating the other parts of a meal. If one of them is sick so that I have to take away or add a special food to help them regain their yin-yang balance, they accept that reason. I think they have an intuitive understanding of the macrobiotic philosophy, that we had to learn the hard way. That's important, because if you're going to stay with macrobiotics, you have to really understand the philosophy of it to get the full benefit. It's not something you can do part-way.

Ginny McEwen and her husband, Bruce, are members of the Ananda Marga Yoga Society, which has a vegetarian philosophy for religious reasons. They have three children, aged one year, five years, and eight and one-half years, who are also vegetarians.

Q. How long have you been vegetarians?
Ginny: We have been vegetarians for about six years. My husband decided at that time for religious and moral reasons to become a vegetarian. To keep the family together, I adopted the same lifestyle and soon realized that it fit in with our whole lifestyle. We felt much better as well. Eggs are not part of our normal diet, although I eat them sometimes. My husband, Bruce, never does. We do eat other dairy foods, but do not eat any meat.

Q. Do you have any hesitations about raising your children as vegetarians?
Ginny: At first I didn't, but waves of uncertainty came back once in a while. The culture is definitely against it — everybody says, "Oh, are you getting this and are you getting that?". My middle child is very picky about what she eats and I worry sometimes that the things she doesn't want to eat are important to a healthy diet. I'm not sure that this is just because I'm a vegetarian — I think all parents probably worry about something like that.

Q. How do your parents feel about your raising your children as vegetarians?

Ginny: Both grandmothers questioned what we were doing but have accepted it. Bruce's father really thought we were nuts and would say so, quoting from the Bible and so on. He went out of his way to make sure there was meat on the table at every meal. He died of a heart attack a couple of years ago. Now when we go to visit Grandmother (his wife), I mostly cook the meals and she'll eat whatever we eat.

Q. How does your pediatrician feel about your raising your children as vegetarians?

Ginny: Once pediatricians have questioned us enough to know that we know what we are doing, they have never said anything else. In California, we took our daughter to a Well Baby Clinic. The pediatrician there was very concerned with protein. I remember her telling us to give Erin lentils, which I thought was strange since I didn't think babies could digest beans very well. She was also concerned about iron intake. They never said anything to us about it directly, but sent us a note every six months to bring Erin in for a blood test for iron levels, without saying why. They never did this with the other children that I know of. We went for the tests and they were always perfect.

Q. How do you feel about your children eating meat?

Ginny: Our kids are allowed to pick whatever foods they want in situations outside the home. Lea is old enough at eight to understand what it means to kill an animal in order to have meat. My mother lives with us and sometimes takes Lea out to eat. Sometimes they will have tunafish, but afterwards Lea gets upset that she ate it. Erin goes to a preschool that has a vegetarian diet so she doesn't come into contact with meat much. We try to keep things that we don't want the kids to have out of the house but will let the kids try meat in other situations. We have taken a much stronger line on sweets, though. I think at the preschool they are also teaching the kids about sugar. Erin came home the other day saying, "I can't eat that, it's got sugar in it."

Q. What were the first foods that your children were fed?

Ginny: One of the first things for all of them was fresh fruit — not pureed, but soft fruit like bananas or peaches. The next thing I gave them was cottage cheese, yoghurt, sweet potatoes and anything I could make mushy without going through a big deal about it. I remember because with our first child we weren't vegetarians yet. Trying to make meat into baby food was impossible. I decided that since it was such a hassle that it wasn't the natural thing to do anyway, so she didn't get meat.

Now that the kids are older, I have to pay more attention to what they are eating. Lea, our oldest, eats exactly what we eat, so I don't worry at all. Erin is very picky so I make sure that the snacks she eats are especially nutritious. She likes to eat mostly dairy products, so whenever she asks for a snack I give her fruit or cottage cheese or peanut butter balls. I make the peanut butter balls from a mixture of peanut butter, whole milk powder, a little honey and tahini, so it's a very nutritious snack.

Q. Do you change anything in the children's diets if an illness comes up?

Ginny: Doctors always recommend going back to liquids when a child is sick. Children want to do that, too; it's only adults that keep trying to eat ridiculous meals when they're sick. Kids seem to thrive on juices or eating fruit or toast. It's a long time before they want anything harder to digest like cheese. When they are sick, I let my kids follow their own intuition. Since we never have junk food around the house, they can only eat things that are good for them no matter what they choose.

Margaret McCasland is a vegetarian single mother who has recently become involved with the Ananda Marga Yoga Society. According to the Ananda Marga philosophy, eating dairy products is acceptable although the eating of meat is not. Margaret has a three-and-one-half-year-old child who is allergic to dairy products.

Q. Were you raised as a vegetarian?

Margaret: No. I became a vegetarian in the fall of 1976. I had been wanting to become a vegetarian for quite a few years, but my husband's family came from cattle-raising country in the west, so he was against it. When we separated, I moved in with friends who were vegetarians.

Q. Do you have any hesitations about raising your child as a vegetarian?

Margaret: I didn't at all at first, because I thought she would be able to have dairy products. When she was seven months old, and was eating a lot of solid foods, she began getting sick a lot. The pediatrician kept giving her antibiotics and claiming it was because she was in day care that she was catching all these infections. The public health nurse at the Well Baby Clinic made the association immediately. When we took her off dairy foods, the infections and diarrhea went away in a day. I have some hesitations about raising a child as a total vegetarian who can't have dairy products.

Q. How do your parents feel about your raising your daughter as a vegetarian?

Margaret: My mother considers herself a health food nut. She enjoys the extra trouble she has to go to when we come to visit. She likes going to the health food store and getting special foods.

Q. How do you feel about your child eating meat?

Margaret: I have found few people who are sympathetic with the extreme diet I have to go to since Annie can't have dairy foods, so I do let her eat meat when she's at other places. I wouldn't want to serve it regularly because I'm worried about the carcinogens and other poisons in meat. But it's very hard for people to feed her because of her allergies if they can't fall back on things they know like chicken. I let her eat meat as much in consideration for them as anything.

Q. Do you have any favorite foods or recipes?

Margaret: Basically, I use soy foods to substitute for dairy foods. I make tofu scrambled eggs and tofu cheesecake and tofu cream pie. In casseroles I use tofu instead of ricotta cheese. I make a lot of dishes using soy noodles with tahini and tofu in the sauce. I make tofu ice cream by blending frozen fruit juice with an equal amount of tofu or soy milk. Then I put the mixture in the freezer for a while to make it hard. It seems to keep for a long time. Another favorite is whipping tofu with carob and molasses and a little bit of cinnamon. This needs to sit for a couple of hours until the flavors blend, but makes a great ice cream substitute. Tofu is wonderful — you only have to bake it lightly or even eat it raw. Annie likes to eat it raw and calls it cheese — its a conscious dairy substitute for her. I also use cooked chick peas a lot — kids love to pick them up and mash them. I am working at a day care center now and am trying to introduce a vegetarian menu, which is working out pretty well.

For breakfast, oatmeal with tahini and brewer's yeast is a staple. I also make pancakes a lot. The basic recipe uses apple juice for a liquid, with a little oil, some tahini, buckwheat flour, a little rye or wheat flour, and wheat germ. Then I add the special ingredients for the day. We like carrot-cinnamon pancakes with carrots grated very finely into the batter. We make potato pancakes by grating potatoes finely into the mix. Grated apples are also very good. We then add baking powder, some honey or molasses, and yeast. If I put in yeast and let the batter sit for half an hour, it makes really high, light fluffy pancakes.

Q. Do you have any other comments about your daughter's allergies?

Margaret: Even if you are allergic to some kinds of foods, there is a whole world of other ones, and an infinite number of meals to make from them if you just try.

Chapter 4

Development and Diet

"Nutrition cannot be separated from the sense of taste."

Maṣanobu Fukuoka in
The One-Straw Revolution[1]

The necessary relationship between internal development and eating habits is usually not described in most baby food cookbooks. This connection can help parents to understand, for example, why some foods are best eaten after ten months of age, or why breastfeeding should take place on a demand schedule rather than on a fixed schedule. The natural timing between the development of a baby's various physical abilities and the growing expectations for appropriate social behavior is truly amazing. For example, the development of good hand-to-mouth control coincides with the time when a baby is expected to begin self-feeding, and it is at this same time that a baby begins to display a strong desire to feed himself or herself. Observing the links between behavior and development can be a special delight for all parents.

The Newborn (birth to one month)

The first item on any baby's menu is, obviously, milk. Most babies need nothing more for several months, because their digestive systems are designed specifically for this food.

The newborn has three reflexes that help bring milk into the body. The first, the oral reflex, causes a baby to turn the head and to reach with the lips toward any pressure applied to the cheeks. (The smell of milk can also help in directing a baby's lips when the breast is near.) The sucking reflex pulls milk into the back of the mouth, and the swallowing reflex passes it into the esophagus, where muscular contractions push it into the stomach.

Digestion begins when the milk mixes with the saliva, which contains a starch-splitting enzyme. There is, however, little time for the newborn's saliva to begin to digest food, because the swallowing reflex quickly pushes the food down into the stomach. In the stomach, hydrochloric acid and an enzyme called rennin curdle the milk, breaking down the large protein molecules into smaller units. Little digestion of fat or carbohydrate occurs, and no nutrients are absorbed while the food is in the stomach.

Within five to ten minutes after food enters a newborn's stomach, it starts to empty into the duodenum, the first part of the small intestine. Although most of the milk leaves the stomach within half an hour, it takes two to three hours before the stomach is completely empty.

Meanwhile, in the duodenum, pancreatic juices and bile continue to break down the milk. One enzyme, trypsin, acts quickly on the partially digested proteins, breaking them into their component amino acids, which can then be used by the body. The primary carbohydrate in milk, lactose, is digested by an enzyme called lactase. The amount of lactase in the digestive juices increases before birth and reaches its highest level during the early weeks of life, decreasing considerably after weaning. In fact, at no other time during life can lactose be as easily and efficiently digested as during the nursing period. To complete the digestive process, other less prevalent carbohydrates are digested by the small amounts of the enzyme amylase, present in the duodenum. Nutrients are absorbed during their passage through the intestine, and undigestible food residues are deposited in the lower end of the gastrointestinal tract for excretion.

To increase the efficiency of digestion, a mother's milk supply varies in response to a baby's needs, which change from day to day. A newborn's stomach can hold only about an ounce of fluid, but within ten days the stomach's capacity increases to almost three and one-half ounces. By one month of age, the baby's stomach can hold six ounces at one time. Likewise, a mother has almost no milk in her breasts when the baby is first born, but her supply increases dramatically over the first few weeks. In addition, the composition of the mother's milk changes as the baby becomes able to digest fats and carbohydrates. As you can see, mother's milk is the ideal diet for the baby.

Formulas can be a satisfactory substitute for mother's milk when an alternative is necessary. However, a few special considerations must be taken if a mother bottle-feeds instead of breastfeeds her baby. Nursing from a bottle requires more control of the swallowing reflex than does nursing at the breast, since the breast's let-down reflex assists the baby by spurting out milk at intervals. This spurting is somewhat controlled by the baby's way of nursing. Small, quick movements bring more milk, and gulping slows down the flow. If you watch your baby closely, you will notice that she or he alternates these movements. When the breast spurts milk, the swallowing reflex works most efficiently and the baby takes in little air. A bottle is not so responsive. As a result, bottle-fed babies will need more burping than breast-fed babies.

Another consideration for the bottle-fed baby relates to milk intake over time. A baby will empty a breast quickly, and spend the majority of time at the breast sucking and strengthening the jaws and mouth. A bottle-fed baby continues to get food as long as she or he sucks, and may swallow more food than is necessary in order to satisfy important sucking needs. If your baby is bottle-fed, you may need to regulate the amount of milk your baby drinks in order to avoid overfeeding. The six to eight ounces that a one-month-old baby usually takes at a feeding can be given in a bottle with a "preemie" nipple, which will reduce the amount of milk that can be sucked at one time. This will extend the time for sucking without increasing the amount the baby is fed.

Contrary to popular belief, taste is not a factor in the choice between breast milk and formula. Taste buds *are* present at birth, and a baby can discriminate tastes at that time, but mature connections between the taste buds and the brain do not become established for several months.

Although I have a bias towards nursing, I do not mean to discourage those mothers who cannot breastfeed because of health or related reasons. As described above, bottle feeding requires a little more thought than breastfeeding, but both will provide the nourishment your baby needs. In either case, if you are relaxed and loving while you feed your baby, you are creating for him or her the beginning of a good attitude towards eating.

One to Four Months

As a baby grows, his or her feeding habits change. The stomach is growing, so the baby drinks more milk. The quantity and quality of mother's milk changes to accommodate the baby's needs. The fat content of the milk increases, slowing digestion and thereby increasing the amount of time between feedings. More complex carbohydrates appear in quantity, and the baby's digestive system matures, producing more of the starch-splitting enzymes pytalin and amalyze. By three months of age, these enzymes are close to adult levels in the baby.[2]

Because digestion is slowing down, and because food remains in the stomach longer, your baby's feeding requests will probably occur less frequently, often at intervals of three hours or more. She or he might nurse longer in the evening, in preparation for a longer sleeping period at night. Your baby naturally develops a feeding schedule suited to his or her needs, eventually approaching adult patterns. Rigid routines are not necessary.

In addition to developments that immediately affect feeding, babies grow in ways that will later contribute to changes in diet. They begin to hold their heads erect, they can control their eyes, and they begin to swipe at objects, making contact with them by the end of this period.

Four to Six Months

By the time a baby is four months old, his or her vision has matured. Your baby now anticipates food when a breast or bottle comes into view. Because depth perception has improved, eye-hand coordination improves greatly. For example, your baby can see you holding a bottle, reach for it, hold it, and possibly maneuver it into his or her mouth. No longer does he or she respond only to breast or bottle closeness; vision has become more important than the oral reflex in exciting appetite.

During this time, you may notice that your baby nurses for shorter periods of time than before — "suck and run," as a friend of mine calls it. Your baby sees new things to explore, and his or her attention doesn't stay focused on eating. Because the breast is responsive to the length of sucking time, the milk supply decreases. This change heralds the need to supplement your baby's diet with other foods, such as yoghurt, juice, and vegetable broth. This is a special time for the father, who can now become fully involved in feeding the baby.

Solid foods, however, are not appropriate. The baby still has poor control over the swallowing reflex, and when fed solids, pushes the tongue out and closes the lips at the "wrong" time, appearing to spit out the food. These actions are not a rejection of the taste of the food, but rather the results of immature coordination, which practice improves only slightly. One mother I know uses the guideline that her child can safely eat only foods that are easily mashed by hand, such as soft, ripe fruits. Preparation involving blenders and grinders means to her that the food is not yet appropriate for her child.

Six to Nine Months

By the age of six months, a baby can eat solid foods. Swallowing becomes voluntary; a baby can hold food in the mouth, spit it out, or swallow it at will. Pancreatic fluid and other digestive juices are nearly like an adult's and are able to digest more complex proteins and carbohydrates. The baby's ability to sit unaided has freed the hands to begin their exploratory development. The hands, as a result, become more flexible and versatile. The eyes and hands are well coordinated, allowing the child to grab at the food he or she is offered. Grabbing, in fact, is the signal in many cultures to introduce solid foods to a child.

New foods should be added to the diet one at a time, with a few days betwen each new food, so that any allergic reactions can be identified. Some foods, such as whole cows' milk and egg whites, still contain highly undigestible proteins which the child may not be able to process until one year of age. However, by nine months of age, your baby will be able to digest beans, grains, cereals, breads, fruits, and vegetables, if you soften or grind them first. A baby food grinder or blender can produce soft, spoonable food, even from raw vegetables and fruits. Christine Ripault, in *Children's Gastronomique,* suggests that you don't feed the more lumpy foods by spoon, but rather allow your child to pick them up with his or her fingers: " . . . if there should be a lump in the spoon-fed food, he is confused. He is accustomed to pushing spoon-fed food back to his throat and slipping it down. Lumps do not go this way, so not knowing how to manage a lump, the baby spits it out. However, if this same baby picks up an object in his fingers and puts it in his mouth, he will immediately begin to chew on it."[2]

It is during the six to nine month period that teeth usually begin to appear. Your baby will probably want to chew on everything and to gnaw, actions which soothe irritated gums and help push the teeth through them to the surface. This is the time to offer "finger foods," such as pieces of fruit or biscuits, that your child can pick up and chew. Please note that finger foods are primarily for practice; they will not form a large part of the nutritional intake at this point. Make sure that finger foods are not too hard, large or sharp, to prevent swallowing problems.

Finally, as a baby's taste buds mature, likes and dislikes become apparent. After the introduction of foods one at a time to check for allergies, you should offer a variety of foods regularly, on the premise that the wider your child's experience, the more easily she or he will accept new tastes and consistencies. It will often take three or four meals for your child to get used to a new taste, so don't be immediately discouraged. Above all, do not force any foods on your baby; you might make him or her reject these foods more vehemently or permanently.

Figure 1

MY FEEDING SCHEDULE
AT NINE MONTHS OF AGE

Name *Shaun Yntema*

Age *9 mos* Weight *19 ¼* Height *28* Date *6-11-52*

BREAKFAST 7 TO 8 A. M.

1. Fruit Sauce—Apple, Prune or Apricot. Well cooked and crushed through a sieve, one to three tablespoonfuls; or juice of whole large orange or after eighteen months juice of half grapefruit.
2. Cereal (cooked) three to six tablespoons. Pablum Mixed Cereal or Pablum Oatmeal (require no cooking). Cream of wheat, oatmeal.
3. Toast or Bread (day old) with Butter.
4. Hard or Soft Boiled or Coddled Egg yolk three times a week. Broiled Bacon occasionally.
5. Milk, eight to ten ounces from cup.

DINNER 12 TO 2 P. M.

1. Broth (clear) or thickened with Rice or Barley, or included in purée of Pea or Potato. Or creamed soups, or 8-10 ozs. of whole milk.
2. Vegetable—Spinach, Carrots, Yellow Turnips, Beets, Peas, String or Wax Beans, Squash, Celery, or root Artichokes. After the second year Cauliflower, Asparagus or Tomato (raw or stewed).
3. Potato (baked) or Spaghetti, Macaroni, Rice, or Hominy.
4. Bacon (broiled) after the *10* month, Calves Liver or Breast of Chicken after *12* month. Lamb Chop or Beef (roast or steak) after the *14* month. Fish after the second year. All should be broiled or roasted—never fried.
5. Junket, Blanc Mange, Jello, Rice or Tapioca Pudding or Baked Apple. After eighteen months Custard or Prune Whip or baked Banana. Occasionally Ice Cream.

SUPPER 5 TO 6 P. M.

1. Fruit Sauce (as given above). After second year canned fruit.
2. Cereal, Rice, or Cornmeal Mush, three to six tablespoons.
3. Toast or Bread (day old) with Butter, Honey, or Jelly.
4. Vegetables after second year.
5. Milk, eight to ten ounces from cup.

No Egg White or Anything Containing Egg White
Before Eighteen Months of Age

Cod Liver Oil or *10* drops of *Poly-Vi-Sol* times daily.

A rigid schedule for feeding babies was more common a generation ago than it is now. Except during illness, there has never been any suggestion from my pediatrician that my son's diet should consist of a list of specific foods. Instead, the doctor asks me, "What is Nikolas eating these days?" and I reply appropriately.

I found a schedule that my parents' doctor gave them when I was nine months old (see Figure 1). It outlines a very structured feeding practice, and shows that I was eating complete meals by this age. This rigid structure is now known to be unnecessary, especially if a baby is still breast-fed. Breastfeeding is more common now than it was when I was young, which may contribute to such a full daily meal plan at so early an age. The pediatrician told my mother to stop breastfeeding me after three months.

As I look at this rigid schedule, so different from the way I feed my son, I realize that my parents must have given me an extra lot of love to balance such a constricting eating pattern. It makes me feel that the attitudes with which parents feed children are at least as important as the style of preparation.

Nine to Twelve Months

During this time, a child begins to move alone, to sit and stand steadily, and to develop finer control of the hands. There is less sloppiness during eating because the child is able to put food into the mouth more accurately, preferring to pick things up with the forefinger and thumb rather than with an open-and-shut palming grasp. My son went through a period of loving peas, because he could pick them up so neatly with his finger and thumb, and could put them clean-ly into his mouth. Such control is satisfying — for the child and the parents.

There is more imitation during these months. Now that your baby has finer body control, she or he can begin to watch others more closely and imitate their behavior. This is the right time to let your child experiment with a cup and spoon while you eat. Your child's interest and imitative abili-ty allow him or her to learn social customs easily. Table eti-quette begins. Remember, though, that eating with the hands is important for babies, even through the second year of life. Allowing your child to use a spoon and a cup does not mean that she or he is ready physically or emotionally to *master* these skills. Above all, mealtime should be en-joyable, not rushed or overly-disciplined.

Again, variety is important. Texture, color, and even at-tractiveness are becoming factors in your child's interest in food, as he or she grows aware of the finer details in the sur-rounding world.

One to Two Years

During the second year of life, a baby learns to walk and talk, and begins to refine other motor and social skills. These new abilities coincide with the growth of a sense of in-dependence and a desire to do things alone. The child wants to explore the things of his or her world more thoroughly than before, and begins to learn from the social contexts of activities. The high-chair and the kitchen are places where the baby can exercise the combined growth of independence and motor skills.

For example, when your child can talk and use his or her hands well, you will have a very eager assistant when preparing a meal. Filling measuring cups, pouring foods from one container to another, washing vegetables and fruits: all of these tasks will develop skills and give the child a sense of true importance. Helping with meal preparation teaches your child respect and love for food and creates a closeness with you because you share that process.

Constructive play with food can continue at the table. Although your child knows how to use a spoon and a fork, he or she will still want to explore shapes and textures with fingers. There is pleasure in pushing food into a spoon with the fingers before the food disappears into the mouth. Cleaning up after a meal can also be a fun-filled learning experience. My son likes to wipe the table with a cloth and dunk bowls and cups into warm sudsy water in the sink.

Once your child learns to talk, a new level of communication opens. Your child can tell you about liking and hating foods. Because imitation is such a strong learning motivation at this time, you may hear your child voicing your own likes and dislikes, ones that you might have been trying to hide. I suspect that this period is often the start of the attitude, "My child hates vegetables." Out of a sense of duty, parents may try to feed a child vegetables they themselves heartily dislike. The child will usually learn to dislike those same vegetables quickly. Vegetarians will probably have much less trouble with this stage than do parents who have only limited vegetable preferences. It has been found that most children *do* like vegetables, and during the second year, much prefer raw vegetables to cooked ones.[4] Vegetarians who enjoy a wide variety of vegetables will probably discover this vegetable "trick" quickly.

Interest in food can actually be created by conversation with the one to two-year-old child. Comparing colors, talking about where the food comes from, and discussing preparation for a meal may help a child try a new food that might other wise be passed up for a familiar one. In general, helping a child to enjoy a meal and to respect the food which is eaten will assure good eating habits and a healthy baby.

As your child observes and imitates you more closely, she or he will prefer to eat what you eat rather than a separately prepared meal. Remembering that your child may not yet have the teeth necessary to chew all foods, you will find this an excellent opportunity to switch him or her to an adult menu.

The early maturing process, both physical and social, is complex and exciting. It is a time to relax and enjoy the changes rather than a time to try to rush a child to the next stage. I have found that even though I welcome the switch to feeding my son adult meals, I feel nostalgic at times for the early nursing moments, for his first taste of yoghurt, and for the sour faces he made when tasting a new food which he always followed by reaching for more of the same food. The lesson that I have learned through watching my son grow is that each moment is special, even if it is filled with frustration, and especially when it is filled with his smiles.

Chapter 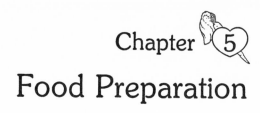 5

Food Preparation

*"Eating should never be an obligation
but rather one of the subtleties of good
living."*

Christine Ripault, in
Children's Gastronomique[1]

Finding the Right Foods

Feeding a young baby is very exciting. You may even find yourself eating foods and combinations of foods that you never even considered before. You will find it helpful to have some basic cooking gear available, as well as to have a stock of foods within easy reach so that your excitement can be based on knowledge and good nutrition.

Most parents have questions about their child's eating habits; I have tried to answer some of these in Appendix A. The best general advice I have heard about feeding a child came from one vegetarian mother who told me that she keeps only healthy foods around the house. This way her children can eat anything they like that they find and she is assured that they are getting something nutritious. If you don't stock the pantry with "junk" foods, there will be fewer battles over eating habits. If you do most of your shopping in natural food stores, a lot of the battles triggered by enticing supermarket displays will also be prevented. When sugar-coated cereals are not in sight, children cannot grab them off the shelves and are less likely to beg for them. If there are nuts and fruit by the check-out counter instead of candy and gum, you will be less pressured to buy unwholesome snacks for the child who is crying while you are waiting in line to pay. Most people find it more satisfying to give their child an apple, a banana or a fig than a chocolate zing bar.

A vegetarian diet is one of the most varied because of the number of grains, beans, vegetables and fruits that exist. If possible, try to grow your own fruits, vegetables and beans, or eat locally grown produce so that you will have a feeling of being closer to the food you eat. There is a good chance that local farmers use fewer mass-production chemicals and techniques than do larger food companies. You are more likely to find vegetables and fruits that are grown without any chemicals, but rather with soil that has been carefully prepared with crop rotation, composting and mulching. Large food producers will take any soil and force food from it by adding chemical fertilizers as the plants grow, after the original planting. Unfortunately, the foods that look the most colorful and shiny clean in the supermarket are not usually the foods with the most nutrients. Plants respond to their growing environment: artificial soil produces artificial foods; natural soil produces natural foods.

A very interesting idea to think about is one presented by the macrobiotic folks: people should try to eat foods which are in season and which are locally produced. Members of the "healthier societies" described in *The Appetites of Man* always eat food by season. Fruits and vegetables, fresh from the gardens, are eaten in the summer. Grains and beans, which can be stored, are eaten primarily in the winter. Even in the United States, people follow a similar regimen: fruits, vegetables, and jello salads are common summer meals, while heavier meals are consumed during the winter. Masanobu Fukuoka, in his book *The One-Straw Revolution*, discusses this issue: "It is unreasonable to expect that a wholesome balanced diet can be achieved simply by supplying a great variety of foods regardless of the season. Compared with plants which ripen naturally, vegetables and fruits grown out of season under necessarily unnatural conditions contain few vitamins and minerals. It is not surprising that summer vegetables grown in the autumn or winter have none of the flavor and fragrance of those grown beneath the sun by organic and natural methods."[2]

Finding basic vegetarian staples should present no problem in most cities. Rural dwellers can either make once a month shopping trips to cities or order supplies from any of the major distributors of natural foods. Some of the more well-known are:

1. Walnut Acres, Penns Creek, PA.
2. Erewhon Natural Foods, 342 Newbury Street, Boston, MA 02138.
3. East West Journal Mail Order, 233 Harvard Street, Brookline, MA 02146.

Kitchen and Cooking Gear

Cost analyses show that making your own baby food is much cheaper than buying canned, processed baby foods. The nutritional value is higher, too.[3] Also, there is not much time saved in buying prepared foods. Most of the meals that I make for my baby take no more than five to ten minutes to prepare. I know exactly what is in each meal, with the added advantage that my baby prefers home-made to canned baby foods. He makes a "gagging-to-death" face when he gets canned baby food in his mouth.

The cost of equipping a kitchen for making vegetarian baby food does not have to be high. You will probably already have most of the necessary items, such as knives, forks, spoons, dishes, strainers, and pans. A baby food grinder and a food mill should also be included in your equipment, as well as several baby bottles and bottle supplies.Optional luxury items such as a juicerizer or blender make a whole category of foods available to you at home, but are not essential for food preparation — I own neither.

EVERYDAY ITEMS

Veggie Scrubber

When you buy vegetables and fruits, scrub them well before use to remove a majority of the pesticides used in growing most crops.

Knives

A good sharp knife is very important for preparing foods. The more finely a food is chopped, the more quickly it will cook. A knife is also good for making bite-size pieces of fruits, vegetables, and breads for older babies.

Grater

A grater is a wonderful device to use to get vegetables to a quick cooking stage that matches the short time needed to cook pre-ground grains and legumes. The large round holes work the best.

Forks

Sometimes forks can be used to mash soft foods (especially fruits) so that not even a baby food grinder is necessary. A fork is also useful when babies get older and do not need foods so finely mashed.

Small Pans

Small pans are good for cooking small quantities of food. If you cook fresh vegetables and there is water left over, save it for the next time you cook grains or vegetables. Many vitamins and minerals are water-soluble and leave the vegetable during cooking, entering the water. By recycling the water, you make sure these important nutrients are not lost.

Spoons

Spoons are useful for scooping food from one container to another. I personally don't use measuring spoons when making baby foods, depending rather on how something looks, feels and tastes to make sure it is ready to eat. This procedure takes a little confidence, but it won't hurt to make a few mistakes to get that confidence.

Baby Spoons

Baby spoons are smaller than adult spoons and fit into a baby's mouth more easily. They also hold less food so that you are less likely to put more into your baby's mouth than she or he can handle at one time. There are spoons with curved handles (easier for the baby to hold, without the danger of a poke in the eye) and with straight handles. There are plastic spoons and metal spoons. Choose whatever you find most convenient.

Baby Food Grinder

This is THE essential addition to a kitchen when a baby is born. No electricity is needed, meal-size proportions are easily made, an ideal consistency is produced — all for about $6. (The price varies from $4 to $8, depending upon where you shop.) Baby food grinders have become popular enough to be available at almost every general department store in the country.

The baby food grinder is a smaller version of a food mill. Any food that has been partially cooked or is naturally soft can be put into the grinder. After fitting the grinding arm and sieve into place, you grind while pushing down, and soon the freshly ground meal comes out the top ready to eat. I usually scrape the food into a bowl, although it is possible to spoon the food directly from the top dish in the grinder. This wonderful appliance can be used for "fast-food" recipes (see page 168) or for transforming adult meals into purees. The grinder prepares enough food for one or two meals at a time, depending upon how much your baby eats.

OTHER SUPPLIES

Food Mill

Most vegetarians will probably already own this item (available through some health food stores for $20 to $30). A good food mill will grind up whole grains into smaller grains, and into powders and flours, depending upon the tightness of the grinder and the number of times you run the grain through. I use the food mill about once every two to three months, each time grinding up a supply of grains and legumes into a rough powder (one time through) which I store in capped glass jars in the refrigerator. These ground up foods keep like flours and can be used to make main dishes within minutes. Simply add three parts water to one part powder. Cook grains until they are soft; cook most legumes for at least ten minutes and soybeans for twenty. (See the legume section later in this chapter.) The three-to-one ratio depends on the temperature at which you cook the grain, so experiment — but keep an eye on it, because it cooks *fast*.

Food mills can also be used to grind up nuts and seeds to make butters. Nothing else needs to be added because of the natural oils already present. However, I advise against making large quantities of nut and seed butters and storing them; the fats in nuts and seeds can become rancid fairly quickly.

Bottles and Bottle Supplies

Even with breastfed babies, there may come occasions when it is necessary to use a bottle. Before my baby was born, I bought three eight-ounce glass bottles with three milk nipples and a bottle cleaning brush. I have since found it necessary to purchase several additional items: a couple of smaller glass bottles, which are easier for him to hold by himself; juice nipples, which are cross-cut to allow coarser material such as orange juice pulp to go through without blockage (there is nothing more frustrating to a hungry baby than to suck and suck without anything coming through); and plastic bottles, which are more durable and practical, especially for when babies reach the age when they begin to move around with bottles and perhaps even throw them, in fun, anger, or frustration.

A bottle cleaning brush is essential because there is no other way to get the milk film off the inside of the bottle, especially if the used bottle sits for any length of time. Cleaning bottles is very, very important. Most people recommend boiling bottles and nipples at least once in a while to get rid of all the bacteria. When you wash bottles, use water that is as hot as you can stand, scrub well with the brush and soap, and rinse thoroughly. It is as important to get all the soap out as it is to get the bottle clean.

A strainer is another useful piece of equipment relating to bottle use. It can somewhat take the place of a blender in making fruit and other drinks fine enough to be sucked through a nipple. I recommend straining something a couple of times unless your strainer has very fine mesh.

Yoghurt Makers

Commercially made yoghurt makers all have one thing in common, an electrically heated base that keeps the yoghurt at the proper temperature. They vary in details like covers and timers, and the design of the yoghurt containers. You can easily make yoghurt without a yoghurt maker; the advantage it offers is the steady temperature, which produces smooth-textured yoghurt consistently. Yoghurt makers cost between $12 and $20 and are available at most department stores.

Blenders and Juicerizers

These are optional pieces of equipment for your kitchen. Cost varies from about $20 for a simple blender to $200 for a juicerizer, with a great range of prices in between. What these electric appliances do is to make available fresh fruit and vegetable drinks for your baby which you might otherwise buy. Blenders make good fruit drinks; a juicerizer or food processor is necessary for vegetable drinks from raw vegetables. Both are nutritious additions to a baby's diet, and some fruit and vegetable drinks can be bought at health food and natural food stores. A blender or a juicerizer would be a nice gift if grandparents were looking for something special to get for the new baby.

Foods: Selection and Storage

There is such a wide variety of grains, legumes, and fresh produce available that it is impossible to cover everything completely in this book. I have therefore chosen to describe some of the more common, easily digested, and easily prepared foods. For quick reference, a chart on pp 138-139 lists the different categories, the major nutrients found in each, and the basic directions for preparing each type of food for a baby. The following pages provide detailed information about the major vegetarian food sources.

GRAINS

Grains are the seeds of grasses, the most commonly known being brown rice, oats, wheat, barley, and rye. Each seed is made of three parts. The *germ,* or heart of the seed, is particularly high in B vitamins, vitamin E, iron, protein and carbohydrates. Covering the germ is the *endosperm,* which is the largest part of the grain and is primarily carbohydrate with traces of minerals and vitamins. The *bran* is the outer covering, providing the fiber that TV advertises so well, with traces of minerals (especially iron), B vitamins, and incomplete proteins. Whole grains are preferable to milled or processed grains because B vitamins, fiber, iron and vitamin E are lost during the milling process.

There are many kinds of grains, each with special strengths, as can be seen in the chart below. All grains are an important source of iron and B vitamins, so very important for the growing baby. They can be fed as one of the first foods, if prepared properly. The important thing to remember is that the grains must be cooked thoroughly for the young baby so that a minimum of digestive juices will be necessary. Preparing grain can either be done by cooking it first and then grinding it through a baby food grinder to make it into a smooth paste, or by grinding the grain into a powder (through a food mill) and then cooking it as needed. Blend the grain with a liquid (breast milk, goat's milk, a nut milk, or yoghurt are favorites) for a smoother, less dry texture. In *Laurel's Kitchen* it is suggested that the introduction of grains be as follows: brown rice (easiest to digest, rich in iron), barley and/or millet, followed by oats and corn, and finally wheat (hardest of grains to digest and most likely to be allergy forming, especially if given to a child under six months of age). Wheat, next to oats, has the largest amount of usable protein, and its germ is the richest source of vitamin E known. In Hunza, the very healthy Himalayan

SUMMARY OF GRAIN STRENGTHS

Brown rice: Brown rice is easy to digest and is a good supplier of B vitamins, calcium, phosphorus and iron.

Millet: Millet has very high iron content, with three times as much iron as any other grain. It is as easy to digest as rice, and forms complete protein when combined with milk. Millet is one of the best sources of vitamin B_{17} and also contains a good supply of B_1 and many trace minerals.

Barley: Barley is a good winter grain since it tends to be more filling than other grains. It is fairly easy to digest and is a good source of trace minerals.

Oats: Oats contain the greatest amount of protein per ounce of any grain. It is commonly found in the form of rolled oats. Oats have a high iron content and several B vitamins, especially B_1.

Wheat: Wheat is high in protein, vitamin E, and vitamin B. It is less easily digested than other grains so it shouldn't be fed until your baby is at least eight months old. Bulghur, or cracked wheat, can be fed a little earlier as a cereal or dinner grain.

Buckwheat: Buckwheat is a primary source of vitamin C complex and rutin (which strengthens capillaries). It also contains a large amount of calcium, compared with other grains.

Rye: Rye contains high levels of potassium, vitamin E, magnesium, silicone, and unsaturated fatty acids — "an important food in the prevention of heart disease." (*Appetites of Man*, p. 67)

Table V
COMPARISON OF NUTRIENTS
FOUND IN 100 GRAMS OF WHOLE RAW GRAINS AND LEGUMES[4]

	Iron (mg.)	Calcium (mg.)	Calories	Vitamin B_1 (mg.)	Vitamin B_2 (mg.)	Niacin (mg.)	Protein (grams)	Protein Quality (percent)
Wheat	3.1	36	330	.57	.12	4.3	14.0	60
Corn	2.4	20	355	.38	.11	2.0	9.2	51
Buckwheat	3.1	114	335	.60	.00	4.4	11.7	65
Barley	2.7	34	348	.21	.07	3.7	9.6	60
Millet	6.8	20	327	.73	.38	2.3	9.9	55
Rye	3.7	38	334	.43	.22	1.6	12.1	58
Oats	4.5	53	390	.60	.14	1.0	14.2	66
Rice	1.6	32	360	.34	.05	4.7	7.5	70
Garbanzos	6.9	150	360	.31	.15	2.0	20.5	43
Lentils	6.8	79	340	.37	.22	2.0	24.7	30
Red Beans	6.9	110	343	.51	.20	2.3	22.5	38
Soybeans	8.4	226	403	1.10	.31	2.2	34.1	61

community, grains are ground fresh daily because vitamin E is destroyed quickly by exposure to the air. If you grind your own grains into a powder to prepare them for fast cooking for a baby, grind only small amounts (enough for a month or two) and keep them in airtight containers in the refrigerator when not in use in order to preserve as much of the nutrient value as possible. Table V is a chart comparing the nutrients found in 100 grams of whole raw grains and legumes.[4]

LEGUMES

Legumes are also seeds, but are found within pods of plants. They include beans, peas, and lentils. Legumes combine well with grains to produce a high quality protein mixture. Legumes also contain iron, thiamine, riboflavin and niacin. Beans are harder to digest than grains, and so should be added later, preferably after eight to nine months. The Farm Community suggests that split pea soup be one of the first legume foods introduced to the baby.

The most important thing to remember when feeding legumes to babies is to cook the legumes very, very well. With longer cooking times, the legume is more easily digested, resulting in less gas. The trypsin inhibitor, which is found in some legumes such as soybeans, is broken down by longer cooking. The trypsin inhibitor prevents the body from using the protein in some legumes.

Ideally, legumes to be used for baby food should be soaked overnight and then cooked in a slow cooker or crock pot for many hours until they are soft. They should then be blended through a baby food grinder, and sieved to remove husks, which are hard to digest. It is, of course, possible to grind dried legumes into a powder much like grains, and to store this powder in airtight containers in the refrigerator to have on hand for quicker cooking. Quicker cooking in this

---

TYPES OF LEGUMES

soybeans	mung beans
garbanzo beans	pinto beans
kidney beans	lentils (red, yellow, green)
lima beans	split peas (yellow, green)

---

case means ten to fifteen minutes for most legumes and twenty minutes for soybeans.

Some legumes are processed extensively (although naturally) in order to make them more digestible. Soybeans are the prime example: tofu is an extremely digestible processed form of this legume with very high protein, calcium, iron, phosphorus, potassium, sodium, B vitamins, choline, and vitamin E content. The soybean does not lose anything by this processing except its relative indigestibility. Tofu, soymilk, and soymilk yoghurt can be introduced into the baby's diet at about seven months of age. Soybeans and soybean products, in fact, are the most balanced solo meat substitute. Soybeans are often the basis of commercial meatless protein foods.

Legumes can also be sprouted, a process which increases the protein and vitamin C content of the seed immensely. Sprouting also decreases the amount of trypsin inhibitor found in raw legumes, making the protein available with little or no cooking. To sprout legumes, soak them overnight in a jar with water. The next morning, rinse the legumes and then continue to rinse them two or three times a day. Cover the jar with a paper towel and rubber band or fine screen to help conserve moisture but to allow fresh air in so the beans do not rot. Within three to four days you will have sprouts.

Any legume can be sprouted. Once sprouted, they can be cooked slightly or ground up raw to make edible and very nutritious food for babies.

NUTS AND SEEDS

This category includes seeds which are all particularly high in fats and oils. Nuts and seeds in their natural form are not digestible by babies, but delicious nut and seed milks can be made by soaking the seeds overnight, and then blending the softened seeds into the liquid which has started to absorb a lot of the nutrients by the overnight soaking. The blending has to be done in a food processor or good quality blender and the food must then be strained to remove any small chunks.

If nuts and seeds are ground up, they make a paste, like peanut butter. If you decide to make nut balls or other taste treats with nut and seed paste, try to grind the nuts fresh; this is not an easy food to save, because the oils become rancid very quickly and can sicken a child. If you buy nuts and seeds, don't buy in large quantities and do store either in the

---

SOME COMMON NUTS AND SEEDS AND RELATED PRODUCTS

almonds	sesame seeds	Ground seeds:
brazil nuts	sunflower seeds	tahini
walnuts	pumpkin seeds	(sesame butter)
peanuts		peanut butter
cashews		other nut butters
pecans		

refrigerator or in a cool spot in an airtight container to retard a natural decaying action.

Nut and seed milks can be introduced in the very early months of a child's life. Pastes can be introduced at eight to ten months of age, and raw nuts and seeds should wait until the child can chew well. Chewing is essential to food digestion of this excellent food source. Nuts and seeds are high in oils, are an excellent protein source, and contain unsaturated fats, B vitamins, vitamin E, calcium, iron, potassium, magnesium, phosphorus, and copper.

I recently found out that it is possible to make yoghurt from nuts and seeds rather than from a milk base. Steve Meyerowitz, in the August, 1979, issue of *Vegetarian Times,* offers the following recipe:

"Soak sesame seeds, sunflower seeds, cashews or almonds overnight and sprout for one day if you wish (sprouting is optional). Blend with 3 parts water for yoghurt. Place in warm area, 80-100 degrees F. for 8 hours with a loose cover. Rising and the presence of air bubbles indicate it is ready. The taste should be tart and sour. You can strain off the liquid and drink it. The strained pulp is your cheese or yoghurt.[5]

FRUITS

Fruits are eaten by just about everyone, no matter what their diet. Fruits are high in vitamins A, C, and B_1, as well as calcium, chromium and some iron. Fruits, or rather the vitamin C contained naturally within them, have the amazing and important quality of being able to increase the amount of iron that a person can utilize. Orange juice, for example, is ideal for combining with an egg breakfast, since the iron in eggs is quite inaccessible except when combined with vitamin C.

Fruits also contain natural sugars that are easier for the body to use than processed sugars. They can also be a good source of extra water and energy on a hot or exhausting day. Fresh fruits purchased in season have a higher nutritional quality than out of season fruits; ripe fruits are easier to digest than green ones, because the high starch content of green fruits changes into simple sugars as the fruit ripens. It is easier for the body to digest sugars than starches. For this reason, very ripe bananas should be the first fruit given to babies, because they are so much more digestible in their mushiest state. Dried fruits contain higher quantities of iron and thiamine, especially the darker dried fruits such as dates, raisins and apricots. They can be prepared for a baby by soaking them in warm water until soft and then grinding them through a baby food grinder.

Fruits should be eaten fresh, in season, raw, and locally produced if possible. Apples, grapefruit and oranges are fall/winter fruits; berries, melons, peaches, pears, and plums are summer fruits. Bananas are not really a local fruit except in warmer climates, but are available pretty much all year round.

When buying fruit, it is useful to know how picking has affected it. The ideal situation is to have your own fruit trees, and to pick fruit when it is ripe and you are ready to eat it. This option is seldom practical. Some fruits, such as apples, citrus fruits, melons, peaches, nectarines, and berries, do not ripen substantially after picking; therefore, if you buy them green, they will probably not ripen enough to feed to your baby. Most other fruits, including golden delicious apples, do continue to ripen at room temperature after they have been picked. Fully ripened fruit should be stored in the refrigerator. The one exception is bananas; cold temperatures damage their flavor.

Although it is certainly preferable to eat fruits and vegetables that are locally grown, there will be times when you may want to eat foods that are grown in other areas of the country or even the world. Bananas, for example, are not grown within the continental United States, and yet they are an easily digestible and nutritious first food for babies. Citrus fruits are not grown in the northern latitudes and yet the vitamins that they supply may make them worth buying, especially during the winter. Two of the major problems with eating foods that are grown outside your area are that such foods are usually not picked at the height of their nutritional strength and that long distance shipping usually detracts further from their nutritional value. However, as stated above, the virtues of some fruits and vegetables grown in other areas may override the disadvantages, especially if the foods are carefully selected at the grocery store.

VEGETABLES

Vegetables are the roots, stems, leaves, shoots, flowers, and sometimes fruits of plants. Although they are composed primarily of carbohydrates and water and contain little protein, they provide essential vitamins and minerals, as well as texture, variety, and color to a meal. Vegetables are divided into three groups: light green, yellow, and dark green.

Light green vegetables provide vitamins, minerals and fiber. They include celery, cabbage, and cauliflower. Yellow and dark green vegetables are the best sources of vitamins A and C. Yellow vegetables also contain the trace mineral chromium. The leafy dark green vegetables are very nutritious, containing calcium, B vitamins (especially folacin, often missing in the American diet), and iron. The darker the green leaf, the richer it will be in minerals and vitamins. Broccoli, for example, is one of the highest sources of vitamin C, calcium, and riboflavin, the B vitamin most commonly deficient in the American diet.

In a study reported in *Organic Gardening* magazine (February, 1979), the following vegetables were rated as the top ten in terms of nutritional value. They are (in order):

1. **Broccoli:** Broccoli has almost as much calcium as whole milk, twice as much vitamin C as in an equal amount of orange by weight and more riboflavin than any other vegetable. It is high in all B vitamins and many minerals.
2. **Spinach:** Spinach has the highest iron content of any vegetable, and is also very high in calcium, riboflavin, potassium and vitamin A content.
3. **Brussel sprouts:** These miniature cabbages are high in vitamin C, potassium, niacin, thiamine, calcium, and iron.
4. **Lima beans:** Lima beans are the best vegetable source of potassium, and are also very high in iron, calcium and B vitamins. Younger limas are easier to digest for little babies, because the starch content is not as high as in older beans.
5. **Peas:**
6. **Asparagus:**   These vegetables are high in iron,
7. **Artichokes:**   calcium, vitamin C and B
8. **Cauliflower:**   vitamins.
9. **Sweet potato:** Both these vegetables are very
10. **Carrots:**   high in vitamin A.

Look carefully at vegetables before you buy them. Leafy vegetables should be crisp and fresh; brown or dark spots indicate that decay has started. In some vegetables, such as spinach, this decay is poisonous to young babies. One reason to buy fresh spinach is that when spinach is frozen, the leaves are not selected with babies in mind. Wash all vegetables when you are ready to eat them and not before; leafy vegetables in particular are usually damaged by

Table VI
(Selected) Foods, Nutrition and Preparation

Type of Food	Nutrition Information	Preparation

Grains
brown rice
millet
barley
breads and
  cereals
 	
oatmeal
	B vitamins, vitamin E
	zinc, copper, iron,
	magnesium, phosphorus
	carbohydrates
	fats
	protein, especially when
	combined with legumes,
	seeds or dairy products
		1. Grind up dry grain in fine food mill until
		   a rough powdery consistency is reached.
		2. Cook three parts water to one part grain
		   until pasty consistency is reached. Cool
		   and season (optional) and serve.
		3. Store excess in closed container in
		   refrigerator.

Legumes soybeans mung beans lentils split peas chick peas	same as grains protein, especially when combined with grains or nuts and seeds	1. Same as for grains 2. Cook in three to four parts water for ten to fifteen minutes. (Soybeans for twenty minutes.) 3. Same as for grains

		(for cooked vegetables only)
Vegetables broccoli cabbage spinach carrots squash sweet potatoes peas lima beans	green vegetables: calcium, copper, vit. B$_2$, C, folacin yellow vegetables: chromium, vit. A and C	1. Cut into thin slices 2. Cook in small amount of water at low temperature or Add extra water to grains and cook with grains until water is gone. 3. Blend through baby food grinder or serve in chunks as baby requests.
Nuts and Seeds almonds sesame seeds brazil nuts cashews	same as grains protein, especially when combined with grains, legumes	1. Grind through food mill until pasty butter consistency is attained. 2. Mix with legumes or rice or serve as nut balls. 3. Eat "immediately": Does not store well over long periods.
Fruits dried fruits (figs, apricots, dates, raisins, prunes) fresh fruits (bananas, apples, pears, coconut)	natural sweeteners vit. C, A, B, calcium, chromium, iron	Dried fruits: Add one or two to grain while cooking in small chunks. Use baby food grinder to blend into food. Can also be eaten raw. Fresh fruits: Don't cook! Mash with fork or baby food grinder or give as finger foods to older babies.

washing and should therefore be eaten immediately before damage turns to decay. Store vegetables in the refrigerator.

When preparing vegetables for young babies, it is necessary to cook them, which unfortunately destroys the vitamin C content to a great extent. Also, much of the mineral and vitamin content is lost into the cooking water. For these reasons, I suggest cutting the vegetable into very thin small pieces right before cooking and then cooking them in as little water as possible (you can always add more). Quick cooking saves most of the nutrients for your baby. If you cook vegetables and grains simultaneously in the same pot, you will not waste any of the water used in cooking because it will be absorbed into the grain. If you cook the vegetables separately, cook them first with only a little water and save the water for the grains and legumes you cook so that it is recycled.

MILK AND DAIRY PRODUCTS

Eggs, milk, and milk products are high sources of protein, B_{12}, calcium, and other essential B vitamins and minerals. Whole milk (cows') often has vitamin D added, which can only be obtained otherwise from the sun. For vegans, the vitamin B_{12}, riboflavin, calcium and cobalt levels of milk will have to be obtained elsewhere, which demands special attention to diet.

There are so many forms of dairy products that it would be easier to look at these types separately:

Eggs

An excellent form of complete protein, the egg is the standard upon which other protein is judged. Egg yolk is usually fed to babies before egg whites because of the latter's relative indigestibility. The egg yolk contains choline, which helps to process the cholesterol in egg whites. Eggs contain iron, vitamins A, B-complex (particularly B_2 and biotin), D, E, niacin, copper, phosphorus, and unsaturated fats. It is usually recommended that egg whites not be given to babies under a year of age due to possible allergic reactions.

Milk

Although cows' milk is usually what is meant by "milk," goats' milk is actually more digestible, being richer in fats and having smaller protein molecules than cows' milk. Goats' milk is less available than cows' milk, however, and more expensive. But since it is commonly recommended that whole cows' milk not be fed to babies under one year of age (because of possible damage to the intestines and stomach by the large protein molecules found in cows' milk), goats' milk is an excellent and actually superior substitute. No milk contains iron or vitamin C.

Yoghurt

One of the most digestible of all milk products, and the one which most closely resembles human milk, yoghurt is made by adding a bacterial culture to warm milk and allowing the bacteria to grow. This bacteria is important for good digestion and proper action of the intestines. Yoghurt is high in B-complex vitamins and in protein, and has a higher percentage of vitamins A and D than the milk from which it was formed, according to the *Nutrition Almanac*. Yoghurt can be made from any kind of milk — yoghurt from cows' milk is most common in the United States, but yoghurt from goat, buffalo and reindeer milk are common in other parts of the world. Dick Gregory, an avid vegetarian, is a yoghurt fan: "The singular exception I make to the rejection of animal products is *plain* yoghurt. Yoghurt is rich in predigested proteins and in vitamins B_1 and B_2. It establishes

---

MAKING YOUR OWN YOGHURT
a simple recipe

1 quart whole milk
4 teaspoons plain yoghurt (fresh)

Heat milk until small bubbles begin to form on sides. Pour into two large cleaned glass bottles. Let cool to 110° (warm on your wrist but not hot). Mix the yoghurt with a little of the warm milk and split evenly between the two bottles. Cap the bottles and put in a warm place (top of a refrigerator, or in warm water on top of a stove's pilot light are good places). Let sit for eight hours and then refrigerate.

---

an acid medium in the intestinal tract which inhibits the growth of harmful and putrefaction-causing bacteria."[6]

Yoghurt can be a part of a baby's diet in several ways. When mixed with enough water to make a liquid, it makes an excellent formula substitute. Adelle Davis reports that babies who are fed yoghurt or even straight acidophilus have fewer problems with such typical ailments of new infants as colic, diarrhea, constipation, and intestinal infections. Ear, throat and lung infections occur only rarely. She further reports that the stools of babies fed yoghurt or related formulas are remarkably free from disease-producing bacteria.

Yoghurt can also be added to grains and fruits for a creamier, smoother consistency. It can be fed as a side or complementary dish at any meal. I give it to my son in place of milk at a meal, and add fruit juice or water for something to drink.

One thing which is very important to remember is to feed a baby only yoghurt which has been made from whole milk. Most commercial yoghurts are made from skim milk, with important fats removed in the processing. A baby needs these fats; it is excessive empty carbohydrates which are fattening in a bad way. In skim milk and skim milk products, the protein is undiluted by the fats and is very hard for a young baby to digest.

Butter

Although butter is made from milk products and contains vitamins A and D, the fat content of this food is quite concentrated and so should be used only sparingly, if at all. It is not advised to fry foods at all for young babies.

Cheese

Cottage cheese, ricotta, and hard cheese are good sources of protein, calcium, fat, phosphorus, vitamin A, and riboflavin. Ricotta (whole milk) and cottage cheese (usually skim milk) can be mixed with fruits for raw snacks. One thing to remember is that almost all commercial cheeses are made with animal rennin, an enzyme obtained from the stomachs of calves. This animal element is not very appealing to the vegetarian. Fortunately, there are cheeses made with a vegetable rennin, although probably they are available only at natural food stores at this time. (I understand, however, that vegetable rennin cheeses are on their way to commer-

---

MAKING YOUR OWN COTTAGE CHEESE

Use very soured raw whole milk that has begun to jell. Hang the milk in a cheese cloth overnight to let the whey drip out. What is left is cottage cheese. Refrigerate it!

In India, lemon juice is added to boiling milk to begin to curdle it. The curdled milk is then hung in a cheese cloth to drop. This type of cottage cheese is called *paneer*.

cial popularity because they can be cheaper to make than animal rennin cheeses.) Small curd cottage cheese is made without rennin, but large curd cheese is made with animal rennin, as is Swiss cheese. All other cheeses can be made with vegetable rennin.

ADDITIONAL FOODS
OF HIGH NUTRITIONAL VALUE

There are a number of spices, natural food enricheners, and herbs which are good for babies (and for parents). Table VII is a guide to the most important. Notice particularly that kelp and other seaweeds provide iodine and cobalt. Iodine is normally available only in seafood and iodized salt. If you do not eat seafood and prefer not to salt your baby's food, it will be necessary to add iodine to your baby's diet. Kelp is the best source. Cobalt is a mineral found in milk products, and is an important addition in the form of kelp or other seaweeds for the vegan who eats no milk products.

Food selection and preparation is a vital and personal part of feeding a baby. I have found that I feel better about the food I prepare the more I know about it. For example, planting and watching broccoli grow, and then eating it fresh from the plant, has revolutionized my attitude towards broccoli. I can now feed it to my baby with much more enthusiasm, which I'm sure he picks up. Knowing how to buy foods makes me very aware of how producers package food to get the attention of consumers. The concern for making money seems to be stronger than the concern for providing good nutritional quality to the public, in many instances. Selecting foods carefully can mean the difference between a wholesome, healthy diet and a low quality, unhealthy one.

	Table VII	
	SPICES AND SPECIAL INGREDIENTS	
Name	**Use - Nutrition**	**Preparation**
Yoghurt	(use whole milk yoghurt!) calcium, protein, B vitamins	• mix with any food • cover foods to make sauce • feed plain
Wheat germ	vitamin E, B vitamins, protein, many minerals	• (nutty taste) • mix with any casserole • can be more finely ground up into flour for younger babies
Nutritional yeast	protein, minerals, B vitamins, B_{12} is often added	• sprinkle into any meal
Tahini (sesame seed paste)	vitamin E, phosphorus, protein, potassium, fats, very high calcium content	• mix with grain or legume casseroles • (seed butter taste)
Bean Sprouts	higher protein than unsprouted beans, B vitamins, vitamin C	• cook with grains or legumes until soft, blend through baby food grinder • mix with raw vegetables in electric blender
Tofu	protein (complete) (high digestibility) calcium, iron	• cook with any meal • blend with fruit or vegetable

Table VII (continued)		
Kelp (and other seaweeds)	iodine (kelp, especially), cobalt,	• sprinkle on food • cook in any casserole
Garlic	may aid digestion	• sprinkle lightly on cooked meal
Parsley	contains large percentage of iron, high calcium content, many trace minerals	• eat raw, dry, ground • add to any meal • use with garlic to reduce garlic odor
Lecithin	phosphorus, B vitamins, lowers cholesterol level	• sprinkle on foods • (eggy taste)
Dolomite (powder)	calcium, magnesium	• sprinkle on foods • (tasteless)
Carob	natural sweetener, vitamin B complex, high calcium, no caffeine	• mix with milk products as chocolate substitute
Honey	Don't give to children under one year! natural sweetener	• use sparingly as sweetener

From: *Nutrition Almanac, The Healthy Family Cookbook, The Encyclopedia of Fruits, Vegetables, Nuts and Seeds*

Chapter  6

Recipes for Healthy Babies

"A well-selected vegetarian diet is in harmony with the laws of nature and will help assure a healthy, vital, and strong body which serves as the temple for our thoughts, feelings, and spiritual essence."

Nathaniel Altman, from
Eating for Life[1]

In the Beginning
(Birth to four months old)

Breastmilk is the ideal food for this age and will satisfy all a baby's nutritional needs if the mother is eating well and taking care of herself. If a baby is allowed to nurse on a self-demand schedule, she or he will take in precisely the right amount needed for optimal growth. A baby will nurse more often to increase the milk supply if he or she is still hungry. This is a natural balancing mechanism between the mother and child so that the baby will not go hungry. The need for a baby to nurse should be respected, although within limits; breastfeeding can drain a mother, especially if she is unable to sleep and rest well enough. The mother's main nutritional responsibility toward her child at this time is to take care of herself.

There will, of course, be times when it is not possible to breastfeed your baby. At these times, there are many homemade formulas which provide adequate nutrition for short periods of time. If you do not nurse at all or if you wean your child onto a vegan diet, it is essential to consult with your doctor to make sure you are meeting your baby's nutritional needs. Commercial formulas try to imitate breastmilk as closely as possible, but often must contain greater amounts of protein, vitamins, and iron, because formulas are not as nutritionally efficient as breastmilk. They cannot respond to a baby's changing needs the way breastmilk does. Since I have a bias against commercial formulas because of their heaviness and smell, I will suggest some homemade formulas which are good for occasional feedings, especially if you vary types rather than feeding only one kind to a baby. Be sure to introduce formulas one at at time, then wait a few days to make sure there is no allergic reaction. Most of the following are traditional recipes and are gentle on babies.

Please note: These recipes are intended only as occasional supplements and cannot replace breastmilk or a complete milk substitute.

HOMEMADE FORMULAS

Kokkoh (macrobiotic milk)[2]

Kokkoh is a traditional Zen macrobiotic milk. There are several recipes for Kokkoh which are used when the mother just does not have enough milk to feed the baby. She is encouraged to eat special foods herself to increase her milk supply, but there is always the possibility that additional milk is needed.

KOKKOH #1	KOKKOH #2
35% brown rice	55% brown rice
60% sweet brown rice	25% sweet brown rice
5% white sesame seeds	5% white sesame seeds
	15% oatmeal

Directions: Roast all ingredients in an open pan at 350°, stirring occasionally until brown. Mix together and grind them to a fine powder (using a grain mill or blender). When cooking Kokkoh, use 1½ teaspoons with ¾ cup water during the first week, increasing to 1 tablespoon per ¾ cup water by the end of one month. Mix well while cooking at a medium temperature until a milk consistency is reached.

KOKKOH #3—special rice cream
1 cup brown rice
10 cups water
¼ tsp. salt

Directions: Wash rice and toast in a dry pan, stirring constantly until it is golden and begins to pop. Cook for about two hours or more on a low flame, stirring occasionally. Squeeze out the cream with a cheese or other cotton cloth.

Nut milks[3]

The following formulas are prepared with the use of a blender and then put through a fine strainer or cheesecloth. Nut milks have been used in many cultures, with a great deal of success. The following recipes were taken primarily from the *Ten Talents* cookbook, written with the vegan child in mind. Where the recipe called for honey I have substituted maple syrup, as honey has been demonstrated to be possibly harmful to babies under one year of age; it can contain botulism spores, according to the National Center for Disease Control.[4]

RECIPE #1
1 cup almonds, blanched (pour a cup of boiling water over the almonds and let stand for 3 minutes to blanch them—this softens the skins and the meat)
1 quart pure water (regular water can be substituted)
2 tbs maple syrup
¼ tsp lecithin (optional—this makes a creamier milk)

RECIPE #2
½ cup almonds
½ cup sesame seed or cashews
1 quart pure water
2 tbsp. maple syrup

RECIPE #3
½ cup coconut
½ cup almonds
5 dates
5 cups water

Nut Milks Plus[5]

Dick Gregory also gives many nut recipes, with vegetables added for extra nutrition. He suggests steaming the vegetables slightly and then using a blender to liquefy all ingredients. Before serving to a young baby, strain the mixture well to remove small indigestible lumps.

DICK GREGORY RECIPE #1

Soy, nut or seed milk (from recipe above)	5 oz.
Carrots	19 oz.
Pure water	4 oz.

Remember! Vitamin B_{12} is not available in sufficient quantity in the plant kingdom for growing babies. If dairy/egg products are not included in a baby's diet, a B_{12} supplement is needed. (See Chapter Two for more information.)

DICK GREGORY RECIPE #2

Almonds, soaked and skinned	2 oz.
Celery	2 oz.
Carrots	10 oz.
Lettuce	2 oz.
Water (use water from steaming vegetables)	28 oz.

DICK GREGORY RECIPE #3

Beets	7 oz.
Carrots	13 oz.
Soy, nut or seed milk	6 oz.
Water	8 oz.

DICK GREGORY RECIPE #4

Avocado	4 oz.
Papaya	9 oz.
Soy, nut or seed milk	12 oz.
Water	3 oz.

Adelle Davis Formulas[6]

In *Let's Have Healthy Children,* Adelle Davis has some more complex homemade formulas recipes, which substitute fully for all of the ingredients in commercial formulas but provide the satisfaction of making them yourself. I have listed the ingredients below; for a complete recipe, it is necessary to check Ms. Davis' book.

ADELLE DAVIS RECIPE #1

The formula base is made from medically certified raw milk, yoghurt made from whole milk, home prepared soy milk, or cultured buttermilk mixed with light cream. To this base, she suggests adding egg shell, a very small amount of magnesium oxide or Epsom salts, some vitamin C that has been thoroughly blended with water, yeast, and kelp, with yoghurt added if the formula's base does not include this last ingredient. She also suggests some optional ingredients such as vegetable oils and lecithin, in small quantity. All the ingredients are blended together very well. The resulting formula can immediately be put into bottles after being strained, and kept in the refrigerator.

ADELLE DAVIS RECIPE #2—Soy milk
Adelle Davis feels that many commercial soy milk formulas are nutritionally deficient, and has developed her own recipe to rectify these problems: Water, full-fat soy flour or soy powder, egg shell, a tiny bit of magnesium oxide or Epsom salts, and yeast, blended well and cooked for at least twenty minutes. Adelle Davis stresses that long cooking is necessary to make soy milk digestible for young babies.

Soy milk Recipe from the Farm Community in Tennessee[7]

Soy milk is a staple of young children after the age of about seven months at the Farm Community. It is important to give extra water to the baby when using a soy milk formula, because the protein is fairly concentrated.
Directions: Rinse 2½ cups whole soybeans and soak in 5 cups of water, for eight to ten hours. The water should be cold to prevent souring. Blend 1 cup soybeans with 2½ cups hot water at high speed, for about 1 minute, or until beans are finely ground. Repeat until all beans are blended.
Pour blend into large pan or double boiler, over medium-high flame. When soy milk starts to boil, turn down heat and simmer for 20 minutes, stirring occasionally.
Pour soy milk through cheesecloth, twisting pulp in the cloth to remove as much milk as possible. Repeat process,

pouring 2 cups of boiling water in with remaining pulp and straining again.

Please note that this soy milk is given as a supplement to the diet; a baby is not fed this formula without receiving breastmilk or solid foods also.

Sikh milk favorites

ALMOND MILK: Take four almonds and soak them all night in water. In the morning, peel them, and blend until smooth with 8 ounces of water and 1 spoonful of maple syrup. Add more water gradually while blending.

WHEAT MILK: Take whole grain wheat, soak it at night. In the morning put a handful into the grinder, grind it, add a spoon and a half of maple syrup and a cup of water. Blend.

Nikolas' Homemade Formula

When I had to stop breastfeeding my son for three weeks when he was ten months old, I developed a delicious, simple formula that was approved by his doctor for extended use. I mixed equal parts yoghurt (whole milk) and goats' milk in a pitcher. I stirred well and poured it into bottles through a fine strainer. Although I didn't like having to warm up the bottles at night when he woke up, I found that he was very satisfied with this substitute. I added the yoghurt because goats' milk has a lower folic acid content than human milk and yoghurt substantially makes up for this deficiency. I added the goats' milk to the yoghurt instead of water to make it creamier and less sour.

I believe strongly that a breastfed baby will not overeat if she or he is able to get loving attention in addition to the nursing time. If your baby seems hungry after nursing, let him or her nurse more often to increase your milk supply. If

	human	cow	goat	ass
Table VIII				
A COMPARISON OF THE NUTRITIVE QUALITY OF FOUR KINDS OF MILK				
protein (%)	1.0	3.5	4.4	1.4
fat (%)	5.0	3.5	4.1	2.4
lactose (%)	6.5	4.4	4.2	6.1
calcium (mg/100g)	28	120	140	81
phosphorus (mg/100g)	14	102	112	47
iron (mg/100g)	.1	.2	.7	.9
vitamin A (mg/100g)	170-670	140	80	60
carotene (mg/100g)	—	—	—	.005
thiamine (mg/100g)	9-15	35	50	60
riboflavin (mg/100g)	28-62	150	100	30
niacin (mg/100g)	66-330	85	400	90
vitamin C (mg/100g)	2.6	NA	NA	NA

from WHO Manual on Nutrition, part 1[8]

this procedure does not work, check with your doctor to make sure the child is gaining weight, or to find out if there might be some other problem which just seems like hunger.

If you are feeding your baby a formula either occasionally or regularly, you will be much more aware of how much she or he drinks. The need to suck and the need for nourishment are hard to separate clearly for the bottle-fed baby. While the breast empties quickly and the baby can then suck as long as desired without over eating, the bottle-fed baby gets a steady stream of milk as long as he or she nurses. You might try nipples with finer holes so that the milk comes our more slowly, lengthening the amount of time the baby can suck without taking in too much food. I suggest watching your baby carefully for signs of fullness and not pressing more milk formulas upon him or her to achieve a daily quota. Babies are very wise and can usually tell you what they need if you listen. Of course, signals can get mixed, so don't feel shy about asking friends or your pediatrician for more specific information if you feel there is a problem.

Ready to Eat
(four to nine months old)

From about four months on, a baby is getting ready to eat solid foods. Fruits, vegetables and easily digested grains are good foods to offer slowly over this time. The order in which foods are offered should take into account digestibility first of all. For this reason, ripe banana is the first baby food of many cultures. It is not only extremely digestible, but sweet, and is a good introduction to the world of food. Avocado, papaya, carrots, sweet potatoes, and rice and millet mush cereals are other foods to offer early. A traditional way to prepare foods for babies at this age in many cultures is for the parent to chew the food and then offer it to the child. In this way the food is partially digested by the mother's saliva, making it easier for the baby to digest.

It is very important to remember to give only one new food to your baby per week or four to five day period. In this way, if the child is allergic to a particular food, you will know immediately which one it is and be able to screen it out until the child is older, preventing a more serious and long-lasting allergy.

Although a parent can feed some foods to a baby at about four months of age, it is not necessary to do so until about six months of age, particularly if the baby is breastfed. By the first half year of life, not only is the child able to sit up and begin to reach for foods, but the digestive juices have matured to the extent that he or she is better able to digest whole grain cereals. Millet and rice have high iron contents that make them ideal foods at this time, since the baby's need for iron is on the rise.

Begin by giving the baby a taste of whatever new food you are introducing. Especially as you start, food should not be fed with the intention of assuaging hunger completely, but should rather be seen as a supplement to the milk she or he is getting. Most babies get very excited by these new tastes and will gobble them down as if starving. This can be a sign of strong curiosity and openness as much as of hunger.

How much you feed a baby at this age depends entirely on how much he or she will eat. There is not reason to insist that your baby eat a specific amount of food, unless there are complicating circumstances that result in a lack of appetite for emotional reasons, or if there is weight loss, listlessness, or other signs of illness. In such cases, it is important to be in contact with a doctor to determine why your baby is not eating and to decide on a plan of action. For normal, healthy babies, however, the amount of food eaten is likely to vary from day to day.

FEEDING GUIDELINES

A rough guideline for offering foods might be as follows (remember that every child is an individual and may be ready for different foods at different times):

• Start by offering very mushy ripe banana one day—maybe ¼ of a banana will be enough.

• Offer banana for the next week once a day.

• Offer another soft fruit, such as avocado or papaya, the next week.

• Vary what you offer. One day give banana, the next day the other fruit.

• If your baby is interested, you might start offering him or her two meals a day: banana in the morning and avocado for dinner.

• If your baby has had yoghurt, you can start mixing yoghurt and banana or avocado together for a meal. If not, you might try introducing yoghurt at this time if you intend to give your child milk products. If not, you might try adding a little nut milk or breast milk to the fruit to change the taste slightly once in a while. This is particularly a good idea if you want to introduce a food that your child seems hesitant about; a familiar milk smell and taste may make it more acceptable. Banana, avocado and papaya are rarely refused by children, however.

• After you have introduced a couple of fruits, you can introduce one of the more easily digested grains, such as millet or rice. Sometimes grains are a little pasty or too dry for a baby. If so, you can mix them with yoghurt or fruit to make a creamier consistency. You can also mix in a little breast milk if you are not using dairy products.

• The next thing to introduce is some of the sweeter vegetables: carrots, sweet potatoes, baby lima beans. By this time you will probably be serving the baby two or three meals a day. You can add juices such as apple or prune juice for a meal-time drink, especially if the baby is still nursing regularly or taking a bottle. If you are avoiding dairy products, this is an important time to decide what you will substitute in the baby's diet for the calcium, B vitamins, and cobalt that dairy products supply in great quantity.

Good sources of calcium are sesame seed milk (prepared like nut milks), soy milk, figs, dates, blackstrap molasses, and apricots. The leafy greens kale, mustard, collards, and dandelion greens are also good sources of calcium, but spinach, chard, beet greens and rhubarb are not. Greens taste a little too strong for young babies; try mixing them with grain.

For B vitamins, use soybeans, whole grain cereals, and brewer's yeast.

Vitamin B_{12} is not available in high enough levels in plant foods so be sure to give a B_{12} supplement if you are avoiding dairy products. B_{12} can be in the form of a powder which is sprinkled on foods, or may be found in nutritional yeast preparations.

Cobalt is found primarily in seaweeds, which can be ground into a powder and sprinkled on foods.

• By nine months of age, your baby can eat almost all foods, with the following exceptions:
  • egg whites
  • honey
  • whole cows milk
  • skim milk

Wait until the child is about a year old before including these items in his or her diet, to avoid possible allergic reactions.

Please note: a vegan baby needs a complete milk substitute when breastfeeding stops. Fortified soy milks approved by your pediatrician are essential to a vegan baby's health.

Table IX

A SAMPLE TIME CHART
FOR THE INTRODUCTION OF FOODS

4-5 months	5-6½ months
Introduce: ripe banana, avocado, papaya, mango, sweet potatoes, and/or yoghurt. All food should be finely mashed or pureed. **Amounts:** single food per meal, one meal a day (breastfeeding still main source of food).	**Introduce:** grains (rice, barley, millet, oatmeal), more vegetables (peas, limas, green beans, squash), more fruits and fruit juices. All foods should be pureed or fork mashed. **Amounts:** one or two foods at a meal, two meals a day, juice for a snack once a day (breastfeeding still substantial).
6½-8 months	**8-9 months**
Introduce: egg yolks, stronger vegetables, such as cabbage, spinach, broccoli, kale, and collard greens. Main meal should be in pureed pureed form. Finger foods should be soft. Presoaked dried fruits and bread pieces are good finger food. **Amounts:** two to three meals a day, or two meals plus finger food snack (breastfeeding at least twice a day).	**Introduce:** legumes, tofu, nut and seed pastes, cheese, bulghur, any other vegtables, fruits or grains that have not been previously introduced. Meals can be in less pureed form, but there should be no hard or large chunks. Finger food can be chunkier. **Amounts:** three meals a day plus finger food snacks (breastfeeding twice a day, especially if no milk products are being given at meals).

There are varying opinions as to when citrus fruits should be introduced; usually somewhere between the ages of seven months and a year.

DAILY MENUS (Samples Only!)

Here are typical month-by-month menus for your baby as he or she begins to eat solid foods.

4 months: Breakfast: mashed banana
               Lunch, dinner and snacks: breast milk or
               substitute formula

5 months: Breakfast: mashed banana and yoghurt plus
               breastfeeding
               Lunch: avocado
               Dinner: brown rice and banana
               Snacks: nut or seed milk

6 months: Breakfast: brown rice, papaya, and yoghurt
               Lunch: carrots and peas
               Dinner: applesauce, millet, and lima beans
               or kale
               Snacks: nut or seed milk, or fruit juice
               (serve milk with meals or breastfeed once or
               twice a day)

7 months: Breakfast: egg yolk, orange juice, yoghurt
               Lunch: cottage cheese with ground sprouts
               and applesauce
               Dinner: barley, peas, yellow squash and
               yoghurt
               Snacks: bananas, fruit juice
               (plus milk or substitutes twice daily)

8 months: Breakfast: oatmeal with ground almonds and dates
Lunch:. sweet potato and spinach with yoghurt
Dinner: lentils, rice, and applesauce
Snacks: bananas and yoghurt, pieces of whole grain breads
(plus milk or substitutes twice daily)

9 months: Breakfast: rice cereal with apricots and yoghurt
Lunch: cottage cheese, dates, carrots
Dinner: millet, peas, mung beans
Snacks: fruit juices, tofu pieces in yoghurt
(plus milk or substitutes twice daily)

—or—

Breakfast: bulghur with brazil nut paste and figs with yoghurt
Lunch: cabbage and split peas soup and pears
Dinner: tofu mixed with applesauce, collard greens and egg yolks
Snacks: cheese and crackers
(plus milk at meals or twice a day)

Eating (nine to fourteen months old)

By nine months of age, a baby is eating on an adult schedule: three meals a day, plus snacks maybe once or twice a day, depending on how hungry he or she is. Snacks that are nutritious and contain no sugar are very important in the diet of a young baby. There is no need to worry about "spoiling a baby's appetite." If your child eats *no* junk food, then you do not have to be concerned about her or him getting enough nutrition; just prepare attractive meals and feed your child with love and pleasure. Nutritional requirements for a baby from nine months of age onward will be satisfied if the following foods are eaten (These guidelines are adapted from *Laurel's Kitchen):*

VEGETARIAN CHILD (eating dairy products)

Vegetables: at least two servings daily, preferably including a leafy dark green vegetable as one of them.

Fruits: one to four servings daily, with dried fruits offered every couple of days (or more often, as desired).

Grains, Legumes, Nuts and Seeds: six or more servings daily. This category includes such foods as whole grain breads, nut ball treats, and cereals.

Dairy: three servings daily. Include breastmilk in this category if nursing is still substantial.

Remember: a "serving" has no absolute size. It is a good idea to have servings from the various food groups be of similar size to assure a good balance of nutrient intake.

VEGAN CHILD (eating no dairy products)

Grains: eight or more servings per day (Include at least one nut and two to three servings of bread.)

Legumes: two cups soybean milk and one to two servings of beans or four servings of beans plus extra calcium.

Fruit: one to four servings a day including at least one raw fruit.

Vegetables: four or more servings per day, including two servings of dark green leafy vegetables.

Vitamin B$_{12}$ supplement

TYPES OF MEALS FOR 9-14 MONTH BABIES

There are five kinds of meals for a baby nine to fourteen months old. They vary primarily in terms of the kind and extent of preparation needed. As a rule, it is good to have one fairly smooth (blended) dish per meal and at least one food that the baby can feed himself or herself. Specific recipes appear on pages 169-179.

Multi-dish Meals

These meals are an extension of the single food approach used with the four-to-nine-month-olds, except that a wider variety of foods is offered at each meal.

"Fast-food" Meals

Recipes for these meals primarily call for preground grains, legumes, and sliced vegetables in various combinations. To prepare, cook all ingredients together until they are soft and not runny. Preparation time is about ten minutes, assuming grains and legumes are already ground to a powdery consistency. If you make a large

Table X

(vegetarian)

DAILY DIET FOR NON-BREASTFED CHILD
(eating solid foods) *

VEGETABLES
(2 servings daily)

FRUITS
(1-4 servings daily)

Yellow

Green

Chromium

Chromium

Calcium

Calcium

A, C

A, C, B$_1$

Folacin

Copper

B$_2$, C

Iron

Zinc

B$_1$, B$_3$

Protein

Protein

B$_2$

Cobalt

Fats

Iron

B$_6$, E

B$_{12}$

Fats

Copper

Folacin

(D)

Calcium

Magnesium

Phosphorus

Phosphorus

Carbohydrates

Carbohydrates

**GRAINS, LEGUMES,
NUTS & SEEDS**
(6 + servings daily)

DAIRY
(3 servings daily)

*Amounts increase with age, rather than with types of foods
Adapted from: *Laurel's Kitchen* (L. Robertson et. al.)

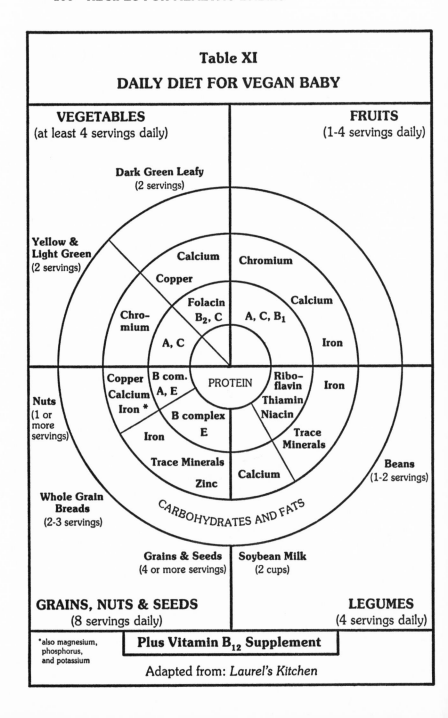

Table XI

DAILY DIET FOR VEGAN BABY

VEGETABLES
(at least 4 servings daily)

FRUITS
(1-4 servings daily)

Dark Green Leafy
(2 servings)

Yellow & Light Green
(2 servings)

Calcium

Chromium

Copper

Folacin
B_2, C

Calcium

Chro-mium

A, C, B_1

A, C

Iron

Nuts
(1 or more servings)

Copper
Calcium
Iron *

B com.
A, E

PROTEIN

Ribo-flavin
Thiamin
Niacin

Iron

B complex
E

Iron

Trace Minerals

Beans
(1-2 servings)

Whole Grain Breads
(2-3 servings)

Trace Minerals

Zinc

Calcium

CARBOHYDRATES AND FATS

Grains & Seeds
(4 or more servings)

Soybean Milk
(2 cups)

GRAINS, NUTS & SEEDS
(8 servings daily)

LEGUMES
(4 servings daily)

*also magnesium, phosphorus, and potassium

Plus Vitamin B_{12} Supplement

Adapted from: *Laurel's Kitchen*

amount, refrigerate or freeze the extra for quick reheating the next day. Don't save foods for more than two to three days, unless the protions are frozen. An ice tray makes a good container for freezing foods.

Adult Meal Adaptation

My baby seems particularly to enjoy some of the dishes which I eat as main meals. The only time that I am hesitant about feeding him from my meal is when I have highly spiced or hot foods, so sometimes I add the spices at the last minute, after removing a portion for him. I used to use a baby food grinder on his portion to make a smoother consistency. As he approached one year, however, he began preferring to feed himself small chunks of my meal.

Blender-prepared Foods

With the coming of age of the electric blender, a whole new food option is available. No longer is it necessary to cook vegetables and sprouts, which actually lose vitamins and minerals in either the heating process or in the water in which they are cooked. Juices and soups (both hot and cold) are the most common baby foods from a blender.

None-of-the-Above Meals

Most baby food cookbooks consist primarily of recipes that appear to consume a lot of preparation time. This approach seems impractical to me, especially as a working mother, since I also need time to prepare my own meals. Since I do not prepare complicated baby foods for my son, I do not have any favorites to recommend. If you are interested in the fancier "gourmet" cooking for babies, I would suggest looking in some of the other cookbooks available. Appendix B offers my review, from the perspective of a vegetarian parent, of most of the baby food cookbooks in the current market. It will give interested parents an idea of which cookbooks might best meet their needs.

Young palates become more sensitive when they are exposed to a wider variety of foods and textures than when they are exposed to foods that necessarily take a long time to prepare. Some of the tastiest foods can also be the simplest to prepare. With a philosophy of simplicity in mind, I have included a section on snacks rather than the more involved recipes which, to be honest, require a parent at home with little else to do than cook.

Recipes

MULTI-DISH MEALS

Since this type of meal consists simply of small portions of several kinds of foods that have been mashed or pureed, recipes *per se* are not included here. The guidelines for a daily diet (pp 163-164) will give you an idea of sample menus. Also, you can put any single food from your meal through the baby food grinder rather than making a completely separate set of foods.

"FAST-FOOD" MEALS

I have divided the recipes in this section into "breakfast, lunch and dinner" recipes, but this is merely tradition, and there is no need to stick to such rigid concept.

Breakfasts

A combinations of grains, fruits and/or nuts make a tasty cereal for a somewhat familiar breakfast menu. Notice that general guidelines are given for making breakfasts followed by suggested ingredients, since all of these foods are prepared in the same manner. I have included only types of recipes that I have actually tried out succesfully with my son. This is a good meal to which you might add nutritional yeast, since the fruit will neutralize the strong flavor.

Cereal Preparation:
1 tbsp. finely ground grain (should be a rough powdery consistency)
2 pieces dried fruits, pitted and chopped into quarters or even finer
5 tbsp. water or nut milk of your choice (see pp 165-166 of this chapter)

Directions: Mix ingredients together, preferably in small (4") iron pot or skillet. Cook at medium heat for three to five minutes, or until grain and fruit are soft. Add more water if necessary; medium heat is different on different stoves. When the consistency is a solid mush, put the food through a blender or a baby food grinder to further mush dried fruit and to mix all ingredients thoroughly. Cool before serving. (Setting the dish in the freezer for a minute will usually reduce the temperature sufficiently.)

Variations: More than one kind of grain can be used, as well as more than one kind of fruit. Add 3 tablespoons of water for each additional tablespoon of dried grain powder that you add, and 2 tablespoons for each additional piece of dried fruit. The general cereal recipe provided the approximate amount my son ate in one meal between the ages of ten and sixteen months. Since appetites vary, you may want to make more or less. If you make too much, you can always cover it tightly and heat it up the next day or serve it cold if your baby likes cold food. (I suggest you do the latter only on hot days. Food should generally be close to room temperature for the baby.)

Another variation includes yoghurt mixed with the cereal to make a smoother, creamier consistency.

BROWN RICE CEREAL
brown rice
pitted dates
almond milk

MILLET CEREAL
millet
prunes
coconut milk

BARLEY CEREAL
barley
raisins (about seven)
nut milk

OAT CEREAL
Quaker Oats or rolled oats
   (not the instant kind)
apricots
kokkoh (see page   of
   this chapter)

WHEAT CEREAL
wheat flakes
ground sesame seeds
   (about ½ tbsp.—
   add 2 tbsp.
   extra water)
figs

RICE & FRUIT CEREAL
brown rice
dried apples or peaches
coconut milk

Lunches

I use the word "lunch" to mean the light meal of the day. This can take the place either at noontime, especially when the weather is hot, or at night, if the noon meal is substantial. Timing depends, of course, on when your child seems hungriest. In some cultures, the morning meal is the largest one of the day. Whatever time of day you choose, here are some suggestions for combinations of food. Notice that this meal is made from raw foods only, which gives it the characteristic of lightness. These nutritious recipes are all prepared in the same way: simply put all ingredients through a baby food grinder. Yoghurt and/or nutritional yeast can be added to any and all recipes.

COTTAGE CHEESE LUNCH
cottage cheese (small curd only—large curd is made with animal rennin)—3 tbsp.
apple, peeled and raw—4 pieces
wheat germ—1 tbsp.

WALNUT LUNCH
banana—½ ripe
walnuts, finely ground (If you crush the nuts under a rolling pin, they will turn into a fine powder.)—5
nutritional yeast—1 tsp.

RAISIN-TOFU LUNCH
tofu—1" square piece
raisins presoaked (Soak raisins overnight in small amount of water to puff them up for easy digestion without cooking.)—8
broccoli, grated (Use finest grater on a hand cheese grater.)—small amount

RAW VEGGIE LUNCH
summer or zucchini squash, cut into small pieces about ½" square—¼ squash
sprouts (mung, garbanzo, lentil)—1 tbsp.
pear, peeled—¼ ripe

PEAS AND TAHINI LUNCH
peas, fresh—¼ cup
apple, peeled, cored—½ raw
tahini—½ tsp.

CARROT-YOGHURT LUNCH
carrot, grated finely—½ medium
raisins, presoaked—8
yoghurt—2 tbsp.

TOFU BANANA LUNCH
tofu—1" square piece
banana—½ ripe
wheat germ—½ tbsp.

HEALTHY WAY LUNCH
tofu—1" square piece
blackstrap molasses—1 tsp.
lima beans—fresh—¼ cup

FRUIT AND SPROUTS LUNCH
pear, peeled and cored—1
sprouts—1 tbsp.
nutritional yeast—1 tsp.

YOGHURT BROCCOLI LUNCH
apricots, presoaked—3
broccoli, finely grated—small amount
yoghurt—¼ cup

COTTAGE CHEESE DELIGHT LUNCH
peanut butter (or any nut butter)—1 tbsp.
cottage cheese—3 tbsp.
applesauce fresh unsweetened,
banana—½ ripe

Other variations—use any combination of:

ground nuts	nutritious "seasoning"—
presoaked dried fruits, or	i.e. tahini, blackstrap
chopped fresh fruits	molasses, wheat germ,
sprouts	nutritional yeast
finely grated raw vegetables	yoghurt

Dinners

I use grains, legumes, and seeds as well as vegetables in my "dinner" recipes. All ingredients must be preground, or in the case of vegetables, finely chopped or grated so that they cook as fast as possible, thus reducing any substantial loss of nutrients. Cook ingredients together with the following amounts of water:

3 tbsp. for each tbsp. grain or legume
2 tbsp. for each tbsp. grated vegetable or equivalent

If the vegetables are finely chopped, cooking time will be about five to seven minutes at medium heat. After the ingredients are cooked, run them through a baby food grinder to mix them well and to even the consistency.

RICE DINNER
brown rice - 1 tbsp.
tahini (½ tsp. to 1 tsp. is all that is needed)
broccoli - 1 tbsp. finely grated or sliced
summer squash - 1 tbsp. finely grated or sliced

Please note: A diet which includes *no* dairy, egg or meat *should* include a vitamin B_{12} supplement, since this vitamin is not found in the plant kingdom in sufficient quantity for a growing child.

MILLET AND BEET GREENS DINNER
millet - 1 tbsp.
cabbage - 1 tbsp. finely grated or equivalent (leaves cook
   quickly)
graham cracker or flour - ½ tbsp. flour or ½ cracker
beet greens - ½ to 1 tbs. *very finely* chopped

MILLET AND CARROT DINNER
millet - 1 tbsp.
lima beans - 7 or 8, preferably fresh
carrots - ¼ finely grated
a little yoghurt added to this mixture after it is cooked makes
a smoother mixture.

RICE AND SPROUTS DINNER
brown rice - 1 tbsp.
mung bean sprouts - 1 tbsp.
green beans, finely grated or chopped—3 medium

SWEET BARLEY DINNER
barley - 1 tbsp.
sweet potatoes - two one-inch squares, finely sliced
fresh peas - 1 tbsp.

GREEN BARLEY DINNER
barley - 1 tbsp.
celery - ½ stalk, finely sliced
parsley - 2 sprigs
baby lima beans - 6 fresh

RICE AND LENTIL DINNER
brown rice - 2 tbsp.
lentils - 1 tbsp. (or a little less)
zucchini squash - fresh, finely chopped

OATS AND ASPARAGUS DINNER
raw, rolled oats - 1 tbsp.
asparagus, *finely* chopped—1 stalk
1 tbsp. nutritional yeast, added after other ingredients
are cooked—1 tbsp.
yoghurt, added after other ingredients are cooked—1/4 cup

BULGHUR DINNER
bulghur, very finely ground - 1 tbsp.
pinto beans - 1/2 tbsp.
beets - finely chopped—1/4 medium
blackstrap molasses—1/4 tsp.

MEXICAN DINNER
brown rice - 2 tsp.
black beans - 1 tsp.
summer squash - finely sliced—1/4 medium
Cover with melted cheese to make this a good finger food.

SPINACH OMELETTE DINNER
egg, scrambled with 1/4 cup milk—1 medium
spinach, finely chopped—1/2 tbsp.
Saute together in vegetable oil or butter for special
taste treat.

BUCKWHEAT DINNER
buckwheat - 1 tsp.
green beans - finely chopped—3 medium
apricots—2

RICE AND SQUASH DINNER
brown rice - 1 tbsp.
acorn squash - finely sliced—1 tbsp.
nutritional yeast—1 tsp

TOMATO SOYBEAN DINNER
soybeans - preferably precooked, or very finely
ground into smooth powder—1 tbsp.
brown rice - 2 tbsp.
tomato - finely blended—¼ medium

SOUPS: There is a quick way to make a delicious cream of
any vegetable soup. Cook several small chunks of a
vegetable (green beans, squash, carrots, cabbage, potatoes
spinach, broccoli, etc.). When vegetable gets soft, add milk,
butter and some light seasoning to the water so that there is
about three times as much liquid as vegetable. Run the
vegetable through the baby food grinder with the liquid, for
a delicious cream of vegetable soup in baby portions. Add
wheat germ or melted cheese for extra nutrition.

ADULT MEAL ADAPTATIONS

Any vegetarian casserole or main meal for adults can be
ground up for a young baby, so I am not including very
many recipes. You can provide your baby with many
nutritious and tasty meals from the enormous number of
vegetarian cookbooks for adults that are on the market
today. Some of my favorites are:
   Laurel's Kitchen by Laurel Robertson - Bantam
   Moosewood Cookbook by Molly Katzen - Ten Speed
      Press
   Tassajara Cooking by Ed Brown - Shambala Press
   Vegetarian Gourmet Cookbook by Alan Hooker - 101
      Productions
   Ten Talents Cookbook by Frank and Rosalie Hurd - self-
      published (College Press)
   Diet for a Small Planet by Francis Moore Lappe -
      Ballantine

The following, however, are some of my son's "most favorites" of my meals:

HUMUS: Cook together soybeans and chickpeas until both are soft. (Cook in a crock pot for 24 hours, at medium temperature. Stove cooking and presoaking cut down on cooking time.) Grind through medium small holes on hand grinder until a paste is formed. Add grated carrot, tahini, a little lime, and garlic to taste. Blend and eat with pita bread. Humus also goes very well in an egg omelet.

LENTIL BURGERS: Cook lentils until soft, but not pasty. Drain excess water if necessary (i.e., if you misjudged how much water to put in—save excess water for next recipe). Cool, mix in 1 egg, and a pinch of garlic, parsley, wheat germ, and thyme. Form into patties, cover with chopped onion and mushrooms if desired, and top with cheese. Put on cookie sheet and bake at 350 degrees until cheese has melted. (Note: A mixture of crushed walnuts and a little soy flour can be substituted for the egg. This adds rich flavor.)

SPLIT PEA SOUP: Cook split peas (green) with carrots, celery, onions, and cabbage until thick pasty consistency is reached. Add wheat germ, black pepper, and other spices to taste.

MACARONI AND CHEESE: Cook macaroni as directed (or if using whole wheat macaroni, just cook with large amount of water for about 10 minutes). Melt large amount of cheese (add more when you think you have enough) with one-quarter to one-third as much milk in a saucepan. Add finely chopped onions. When cheese sauce is melted, add fresh peas and pour over macaroni. Mix well. Cover with wheat germ, parsley, and grated cheese. Bake at 350° until cheese is melted.

BLENDER-PREPARED FOODS

Because the availability of fresh fruits and vegetables varies with the season, I have included here only general recipe guidelines for blender foods. Blackstrap molasses, nutritional yeast and wheat germ can be added for extra nutrition. Milk and yoghurt can be added for more of a milkshake consistency. Nut milks and coconut add extra body.

VEGETABLE JUICES: Mix any two vegetables with a little water until completely blended. (Using too many vegetables at one time covers up the taste of most). Carrots, cabbage, celery, tomatoes, beets, and watercress are especially good for vegetable juices.

FRUIT JUICES: Almost any fresh fruit can be combined or taken alone, with water or milk (goats' or nut milk, preferably) to thin it down. Add nutritional yeast for a nutritional treat.

FRUIT AND VEGETABLE JUICES: Some fruits and vegetables can be combined for a surprisingly good taste, such as: cabbage and cantaloupe, orange juice and carrots, beets and watermelon.

SOUPS: To make soups, use less water than normal for a thicker consistency. Soups can be hot or cold (but to neither extreme for a baby). Whole grain breads can be soaked in the soup if the child can't or doesn't want to eat the soup alone.

SPROUT DRINKS: Because bean sprouts are so small and require good chewing for proper digestion, blending them with other vegetables or fruits is an excellent way to add nutrition to your baby's diet.

SNACKS AND OTHER FOODS

Snacks come in two varieties: those that take only a couple of minutes to prepare and those that take longer. In the first category, here are some nutritious goodies:

• Any dried fruit (For children over nine to ten months old. Make sure you keep an eye on your baby with this snack.)

• Chunks of fresh fruit (Fruit should be ripe so that there will be no danger of choking or indigestion.)

• Chunks of fresh fruit covered with yoghurt (A messy snack, but delicious!)

• Hard boiled eggs (Without the shells, naturally. For children under a year, hard boiled egg yolks should be given alone, without the whites.)

• Apples dipped in any nut butter (Any nut can be ground in a fine hand grinder to make a nut butter. The grinding, if it is fine enough, creates enough oil to make a paste.)

• Carrots dipped in nut butter or cottage cheese

• Pieces of cheese

• Any whole grain bread (small chunks) covered with nut butter

• Crackers with nut butter and yoghurt mixed

• Cooked beans (This makes a nice finger food.)

• Any cooked vegetable, plain or covered with yoghurt

• Nut balls (Mix together equal parts of nut butter, carob powder, instant milk, honey and wheat germ; divide into small lumps or balls.)

• Homemade popsicles (Freeze orange juice or any fresh fruit juice—except pineapple, which does not freeze well. Pour it into small paper cups and insert popsicle sticks or wooden spoons, which can be reused. Freeze until juice is solid. Remove cup by holding stick and running under hot water for about ten seconds. Another good popsicle can be made by blending yoghurt with any fruit juice and freezing the mixture as described above. Homemade popsicles are very good for teething babies, as they soothe sore gums.)

• Cold pancakes: Serve leftover pancakes for a snack. Here is the basic recipe:

1½ cups flour (as much as ¾ cup whole wheat or
   soy flour)
1 tsp. salt
1¼ tsp. baking powder

Mix the above ingredients together.

Beat two eggs together. Add 1½ cup milk. At this point add as much mashed fruit as desired—up to about a cup. Bananas are a favorite.

Stir egg mixture into dry ingredients mixture.

Add up to ¼ cup oatmeal, very finely crushed nuts, or any grain powder.

Yoghurt can be added instead of about ½ cup milk.

Cooking directions: Cook pancakes on hot skillet. Cover with yoghurt instead of maple syrup if desired.

Growing up (twelve to twenty-four months old)

By twelve to fourteen months of age, babies are beginning to feed themselves and can pretty much eat whatever you are eating at a meal, as long as your foods are not too highly spiced (remove a small portion before you spice the foods with strong herbs), and as long as the foods are not too hard (for example, casseroles with nuts should be well baked to soften the nuts). Switching to an adult fare depends on your child's interest and number of teeth. Without several upper and lower teeth in, a baby will still need to have food finely chopped or ground in the baby food grinder.

Therefore, rather than including recipes for this age, it would be better to refer you to a vegetarian cookbook for adults, such as the ones listed in the previous section. By now, what you are eating should be healthy enough that you will not have to think about what to feed your baby. Consulting the daily food guides on pp 165-166 will help you determine whether you and your child are eating the well-balanced diet which your growing child needs.

Conclusion

Writing a book for parents to help them to more confidently raise a vegetarian baby has been very exciting but also very difficult. I could not possibly include everything that a parent might want to know about raising a vegetarian baby, because helping a child grow into a healthy adult is a much broader area than feeding a vegetarian baby. I couldn't include everything I wanted on child development. Another area that I was not able to cover is the vegetarian child after age two. I deliberately limited the scope of this book because I felt that after a child is eating adult meals with his or her parents all the time, the parent's diet becomes the major concern rather than the child's, and the adult vegetarian diet is explained in many other books. I would like to remind parents, however, that diet "supplements" such as nutritional yeast, a pinch of kelp every other day or so, and wheat germ, are really essential parts of the diet of any vegetarian child, age 7 months or 4 years, or 12 years. A tablespoon of nutritional yeast mixed into orange juice will fulfill the majority of a child's RDA for all B vitamins, including B_{12}, and will be a favorite drink of the older child if she or he has had it since 6 or 7 months of age. It can become a favorite with children who did not start out on it as well: a friend of mine says she gets "cravings" for it, probably when her diet needs a special boost. Adding such essential supplements regularly will also prevent the body from running down as quickly if the child should stop eating from sickness at some point. Prevention is really the best way to raise a healthy vegetarian baby.

The main point I would like to stress is that there is a natural development in babies that can make a parent's job easier. If you watch carefully, you will notice that your baby will tell you what he or she needs and often can help you with the timing of introducing a spoon or a cup or finger foods or whatever the next step may be. Your responsibility as a parent, as Clara Davis, in her study of the self-selection of diets in young children strongly suggests, is to offer nutritious, well-balanced foods, in a friendly relaxed atmosphere. George Ohsawa, who brought macrobiotics to this country, correctly implied that parents need to think about their own development in order to raise children as best they can. A parent who has made the effort to educate herself or himself adequately on vegetarian nutrition for babies, and who has spent some energy figuring out what is truly important in life and living with those principles in mind, will make a very good parent. A relaxed, healthy baby will be the natural result of such an environment.

Appendix A

Questions and Answers

This section exists in response to the many people with whom I have talked informally about raising vegetarian babies. My answers to their questions provide information that was not thoroughly covered in any other section of the book.

Q. How can you raise your children as vegetarians if they don't like vegetables? I thought children usually don't like vegetables, especially when they're young.

A. The concept of a "vegetable war" is a common one among meat eaters. In fact, there was an article in the September, 1978 issue of *American Baby* magazine entitled: "Kids vs. Vegetables: How to Win the War." I think the stereotype of children hating vegetables is derived from two sources. First, many parents do not like vegetables very much and convey this message to their children even as they are trying to force vegetables on them "because it's good for them." The second factor is that most meat eaters prepare vegetables only as a side dish and usually do not put the attention into making the food taste good the way that a vegetarian would. No one likes overdone, soggy vegetables — which also, by the way, have lost a good deal of their nutrients through overcooking.

If you give your child food you enjoy — fresh vegetables, not overcooked, at times lightly seasoned or mixed with yoghurt — I doubt that a "vegetable war" will ever occur. War exists only if someone is fighting. If parents don't force their children to eat vegetables, sooner or later the children will enjoy eating most vegetables. Dr. Gesell, in his book, *Feeding Behavior in Infants,* notes that children during the second year of life prefer raw to cooked vegetables; this preference should certainly be encouraged. I would like to see parents openly sharing their love for vegetable foods with their children.

Q. What do I do if my child refuses to eat the foods I prepare? How do I make sure she or he eats enough to get the RDA of all vitamins and minerals?

A. The first thing to do is to figure out why your child isn't eating. There are three probable reasons:

1. Your child is sick, in which case you should respect her or his feelings about how much food to eat. You might try offering more soupy or light foods rather than concentrating on a normal meal.

2. Your child may not be enjoying mealtimes. Is the eating atmosphere calm and happy? Are *you* as a parent enjoying these times?

3. Your child is becoming more of an individual person. Experimenting with likes and dislikes of certain foods may be part of this development. This experimentation usually hapens during the second year of life. It is helpful not to make a fuss over it. Serve more of a variety to replace something the child is temporarily refusing to eat, and above all, make sure that you are not serving empty calorie foods that will take away the child's ap-

petite. Snacks are useful, especially if the child is not eating large amounts at meals, but make sure those snacks are very nutritious (see recipe section on snacks, Chapter Six, p. 179).

If your child is offered nothing but tasty, nutritious foods, there is no need to worry when a period of food refusal or a preference for certain foods comes along. Dr. Clara Davis' study of self-selection of diets in children as described in Chapter One of this book supports this view.[2]

An alternative to offering snacks to the child who is not eating well is to offer only two or three meals a day, and at those meals, to serve nutritious snack type foods that contain a good balance of essential nutrients.

Q. What about vitamin supplements?

A. Vitamin supplements are unnecessary unless one of the following conditions exists:

1. You live in a very cloudy area so that your child is not exposed to sunlight for any substantial part of the year. In this case, a *vitamin D supplement* is highly recommended.

2. Your child is eating no dairy or meat products at all (including yoghurt, eggs, and milk). In this case, a *vitamin B_{12} supplement* is warranted. Also, in the case of a vegan child, unless a substantial amount of green leafy vegetables and/or sesame seed preparations are consumed, a *calcium supplement* may be necessary to assure proper bone and tooth development.

3. If your child is sick or for some reason unable to get enough of some nutrient from the offered diet to stay healthy, other supplements may be recommended. An iron supplement, for example, may be recommended for an anemic baby. Unless your baby is anemic, however, an iron supplement is not necessary. Some obvious signs of anemia are pale skin and, in normally energetic babies, constant lack of energy. Since cows'

milk does not contain iron, a baby who is drinking a lot of milk to the exclusion of iron rich foods such as whole grains may develop anemia and will need an iron supplement. (See Chapter Two, p. 54 on iron for more iron-rich foods.)

Q. How should I approach our pediatrician about my baby's vegetarian/vegan diet?

A. It would be nice if all doctors felt comfortable about a vegetarian/vegan diet, but unfortunately this is not the case. It is worth looking around for a sympathetic doctor, especially if you live in a well-populated area. However, the chances are that your pediatrician is not particularly knowledgeable about the vegetarian/vegan diet and may therefore be a little wary of it. I think the best approach is a knowledgeable one: know the basics of vegetarian nutrition and share these with your doctor in a friendly way. If the doctor gets the sense that you are being careful about what you are doing, she or he will probably be much more accepting. If you are told that "all babies must be given iron supplements," for example, suggest giving iron-rich natural foods as an alternative. If the doctor still balks, then you need to make the ultimate decision. I recommend telling the doctor in a friendly, open way, if you choose not to follow his or her directions. It is hard not to feel on the defensive if you disagree with the medical profession, but if you have thought out what you are doing and why, and if you are really able to listen to the doctor's point of view, you should be able to make an educated decision with or without your doctor's support. The reason I recommend your telling the doctor when you choose an alternative to his or her recommendation is to demonstrate that a successful alternative exists. (And, in the improbable case that difficulties do arise, he or she will have more information with which to remedy the situation.)

Q. What do I do if my baby is offered meat?

A. This is entirely a personal decision, depending upon how strongly you feel about not eating meat, how much you want to shape your child's opinions, and how well you are able to respond to a meat-eating culture. If you have been able to make a vegetarian stand with your families and friends, there will be fewer situations arising in which your child is offered meat. You may choose to regulate strictly the environment of your child (i.e., avoid meat eaters in action) until he or she is old enough to talk and think about the issue. I personally believe that a child eventually will arrive at a similar dietary philosophy. I prefer not to interfere directly with the process of making such a decision, but rather to use a more indirect approach of limiting my son's exposure to meat, at least while he is young. It is an issue similar to that of "TV or not TV."

Q. When should I start making sure my baby's teeth are cleaned? Are children on a vegetarian diet less likely to get cavities?

A. Cavities (dental caries) are created by prolonged exposure to sugar. No amount of fluoride in the water or as a supplement will prevent cavities in the child who eats a lot of sugar products. However, there are hidden cavity causers even among natural foods: dried fruits, for example, are terrible for teeth because they are so sticky and therefore stay on the tooth longer than the sugar in fresh fruits. The longer sugar in any form stays in contact with a tooth, the longer the active bacteria in the saliva have to eat away the tooth enamel and into the tooth, causing decay. (The bacteria that cause tooth decay thrive on sugar.) However, dried fruits should not be excluded from the diet, since they do contain valuable minerals and vitamins along with the sugar. It helps to give the child abrasive foods after or even with dried fruits. For example, nuts, even ground somewhat, will help remove sticky fruit, which is one reason a nut and fruit mixture is a good snack. Raw apple is also a good after-meal tooth cleanser. DeVore and White report that "Some dentists feel that eating a slice or two of raw apple after a meal not only removes particles of food from between the teeth but also stimulates the gum tissues and actually reduces tooth decay by causing a salivary flow."[1] Sugar cane is another less common snack that is both sweet but abrasive enough to clean the teeth as it is chewed. DeVore and White report in their book, *Appetites of Man,* that in the Marquesan Islands, "The children all chew on sugar cane and carry a piece to school with them to supplement their school lunch."[2] They go on to say that before processed sweets were introduced into the Marquesan diet, the islanders were believed to be completely free of dental caries. The vegetarian Hunza of the Himalayas also have a carie-free life. DeVore and White tell us, "The children have perfect teeth and well-formed dental arches. They clean their teeth with small twigs and have no idea what toothpaste is for."[3] Carrots, celery and other raw vegetables have been found to have a similar cleansing effect.

Besides omitting processed sugars and sugar foods from the diet, getting sufficient calcium and magnesium is vital for producing strong and healthy teeth. This need begins before birth, since several front teeth begin to form their roots during the fourth or fifth month of pregnancy. If the calcium supply is too low in babies, their teeth will be more susceptible to decay for the rest of their lives.

Generally, a healthy diet promotes strong teeth. DeVore and White report that "it was found that when the body is in perfect mineral balance, saliva has defensive factors that control the growth of bacteria in the mouth. Successful new preventive measures are being taken by some dentists to adjust their patients' body mineral balance, and thus inhibit decay. Of course, sugar is prohibited in the diet."[4]

If a good diet is eaten, and if care is taken to provide abrasive and fibrous foods with sticky foods, there is little chance that you will have to be concerned about your child developing caries. An additional idea deals with the introduction of the toothbrush. Since it will be almost impossible to limit totally your child's processed sugar intake as she or he gets older, it is important to teach proper dental care which involves the use of a toothbrush. When he was a year old, my son liked to chew on a toothbrush while he was in the bathtub before bed. During teething, he semed to enjoy the massage that a toothbrush gives. Sometimes I brush my teeth with him, which he also enjoys since we are doing the same thing. I always brush my teeth dry first, and then use toothpaste for the mouth-freshening effect. Through enjoyable imitation, he is beginning to use good dental care. Some say that parents should use cotton and clean their baby's teeth once a day, but that would just not work for me; Nikolas has never liked having my hands in his mouth. I feel satisfied with this alternative.

Q.What about feeding a sick child?

A.Depending upon the sickness, of course, a sick child will not want or need many solid foods. Grains and legumes are often too heavy to digest for the body which is trying to heal itself. Fruit, vegetable and sprout drinks and soups are usually much more acceptable to the baby, both physically and psychologically. Whole grain bread is often digested well, and will provide strengthening nutritional value to a sick child's diet. Above all, believe your child when she or he doesn't want a lot to eat. If your child seems to be getting well but is still not eating, feed him or her small amounts of packed nutrition (see Snacks section). The less one eats, the more accustomed one becomes physically to eating small amounts, so gradually increase the amount of food you offer a child who is getting well.

Q.I have heard that milk is mucous-forming. Does this mean that I should limit the amount of milk I give my baby?

A. The relationship between milk and mucous has been explained best by Dr. Rudolph Ballentine, in his book called *Diet and Nutrition*. He relates the two terms to an Eastern Indian system of health called Ayurveda, meaning "the science of life." He explains:

"Milk is a body builder. It is designed to be the most efficient food possible for the rapidly growing animal. In Ayurvedic terms, milk is said to promote 'Kaph.' This is the solid, substantial aspect of the human being, and when it is deficient, one is likely to be unstable psychologically, and thin and underdeveloped physically. During periods of growth, when recovering from an illness, or when one needs to gain weight, milk can be a very valuable addition to the diet. If the body does not need to increase in 'Kaph,' however . . . then it is thrown off as waste . . . unusable 'Kaph' is what is known in the west as mucous."[5]

Since mucous can also result from other than excess kaph, this does *not* mean that milk should be removed from the diet of a baby with a cold. In fact, a cold being an illness, kaph is needed to maintain the body's health. Other foods which are said to increase kaph are carrots, summer squash, garbanzos, mung beans, kidney beans, radishes and dill greens.

Q. I don't want to give my child any dairy products, but he is a picky eater and I'm worried that he won't get enough protein. What can I do?

A. When a child does not eat dairy products or eggs at all, it is of utmost importance that everything the child eats be nutritionally sound. Since it does take more plant food to equal the amount of protein found in meat, it may be necessary to offer the vegan child more small meals of special high protein snacks.

I would suggest breastfeeding the vegan child for at least a year, to assure that a basic complete protein is available to the child. During the later part of the first year, it is important to introduce a fortified soymilk. At the Farm, a vegan community in Tennessee, a soy milk dairy has been set up, which adds vitamin B_{12}, A and D to the milk. Adelle Davis also suggests adding some calcium from eggshells crushed into a powder, and magnesium to the milk as well. Commercial soy formulas can also be used, although a recent Associated Press news item stated that Neo-Mull-Soy and Cho-Free, two soy formulas, are being recalled by their manufacturer because they have been found to cause a salt-deficiency illness (August 3, 1979, Washington AP report). If you need to feed your baby a soy formula instead of breastfeeding, you should consult with your doctor or contact the people at the Farm for more complete information. (The Farm, 156 Drakes Lane, Summertown, Tenneseee 38483.) One advantage of introducing a soymilk or soy formula before the end of the first year is that the taste is strong and as a child develops strong likes and dislikes in foods this taste may cause some balking. After the child is eight months old, high protein foods such as tofu, nuts and ground seeds, and beans can be added to the diet. Tofu has a high protein content and should be fed with liquid in the same meal to aid complete digestion. Tofu, soymilk and nut yoghurts can be prepared in a variety of ways — with fruits or carob to increase attractiveness to the picky eater. Carob is an excellent substitute for chocolate, being rich in vitamins A and B-complex, as well as containing a good supply of calcium, phosphorus, magnesium, iron, copper and other trace minerals. It also contains some protein and carbohydrates and, unlike most commercial chocolate, contains no sugar. *The Encyclopedia of Fruits, Vegetables, Nuts and Seeds,* by Joseph Kadans, reports that carob flour is sometimes beneficial in cases of diarrhea where there is no specific bacteria or other disease present, and has been added to formulas for babies who have trouble with digestion.[6]

With soy foods, nuts and seeds, and legumes as a basic part of the vegan's diet, there should be no problem with adequate protein intake. Variety and attractiveness of foods as well as a good attitude on the part of the parents will assure a healthy vegan child.

I would like to extend an invitation to vegetarian and vegan parents to send me comments and questions, particularly in the case that this book is expanded at some future time. I feel strongly that the sharing of information among parents is one of the best ways for us all to learn.

Reviews of Baby Food Cookbooks

Another Little Mouth to Feed, by Florence Rogers, Simon and Schuster, 1973, 168 pp. ($3.95)

Vegetarians are forgotten in this all-American diet (complete-with-a-dessert-section) baby cookbook.

The Baby Food Book, by Alma Payne, Little Brown and Co., 1977, 161 pp. ($3.95)

A nutrition book that thanks Gerber and Beech-Nut Baby Food Companies in the acknowledgements, this is a strange assortment of information — often incorrect, but sometimes useful. For example, this is one of the few baby food books that includes a section entitled, "For the Baby of Vegetarian Parents;" yet that section makes it sound as though vegetarian parents are a little wacky, if not actually risking their babies' health. Payne suggests, incorrectly, that the vegetarian diet should have salt added to it to "counteract the amount of potassium in a high carbohydrate diet" (p. 105). She feels that raw milk is bad — "the simple truth is it is not safe for baby (or anyone else)" — and explains how to sulfurize fruit. She also denigrates the vegan diet, saying

"The pure Zen Macrobiotic diet is a killer and no one should be on it" (p. 107). She obviously has included the section for vegetarians without properly doing her homework. Her descriptions of how tasty meat is are somewhat nauseating.

On the other hand, this book does contain some good nutritional information, a section on vegetarian main dishes, and a section on how to dry vegetables.

Baby Gourmet Book, by Mary Fisk, Determined Productions, 1978, 127 pp. ($5.95)

This is unfortunately a meat, white flour and sugar recipe book, although very attractively illustrated.

Baby's Recipe Book, by Linda McDonald, A. S. Barnes and Co., Inc., 1972, 122 pp. ($3.95)

This is one of the better baby food books available. It includes nutrition and practical preparation information for children on meat-based diets, vegetarian diets, wheat-free diets, egg-free diets and milk-free diets as well as information on food preservation and menu planning. My only quibble with this book is its reliance on textured, processed vegetable proteins (Vegelone, Nutreena, Vegeburger, etc.) rather than on unprocessed "natural" foods for the vegetarian diet.

Better Food for Better Babies, by Gena Larson, Keats Publishing Co., 1972, 108 pp. ($1.25)

This natural foods recipe guide for babies contains a few vegetarian main dishes for the whole family which can also be served to older infants. Although the book is primarily intended for meat-eaters, the author does not convey a strong meat-eating-is-necessary-for-your-baby's-health message. She does not discuss nutrition as such, but presents recipes with some generalized guidance based on sound nutritional information. Sections are included on a mother's prenatal diet, on making cottage cheese and yoghurt, on sprouting foods, and on how to make festive colored foods safely (beet juice for pink, very fine parsley or spinach for green, raw carrots for yellow).

Children's Gastronomique, by Christine Ripault (translated by Charlotte Turgeon), Crown Publishing Co., 1968, 364 pp. ($5.95 cloth)

Advertising itself as a "French gourmet cookbook for babies and young children," this is a complete and enjoyable book for parents of *non*-vegetarian babies. It includes nutrition information, meal-planning, recipes, advice by "specialists" (doctors, a dietician, a psychologist, and a director of infant nurseries). Stress is given to simple tasty meals. Recipes are categorized according to a baby's length and body weight. Unfortunately, vegetarians are not mentioned. There is a very small section on legumes which is supportive, but sometimes inaccurate, probably because vegetarian staples are not often found in gourmet French cooking.

Feed Me, I'm Yours, by Vicki Lansky, Bantam, 1977, 150 pp. ($1.95)

This book describes how to make your own baby food, but is based on a meat diet, with some strange ideas such as giving the six- to eight-month-old such finger foods as "mashed potato, Cheerios, ice cream and applesauce." Lansky usually recommends honey instead of sugar, but suggests processed foods such as marshmallows, jello and candy corn in "special treats." Starting a young baby on such high sugar foods is sure to create an unwanted sweet tooth.

The First Baby Food Cookbook, by Melinda Morris, Grosset and Dunlap, Inc., 1972, 118 pp. ($4.95 cloth)

This "gourmet" recipe book for babies is attractive, but contains no nutrition information, and uses meat as its basis. Morris often suggests adding sugar to recipes. The book is available only in hardcover.

Instant Baby Food, by Linda McDonald, Oaklawn Press, 1977, 108 pp. ($3.95)

Linda McDonald is an avid fan of the baby food grinder, as am I, so I tend to like her book, although the vegetarian baby is not mentioned in it. She does mention beans in one paragraph in the book.

Making Your Own Baby Food, by Mary and James Turner, Bantam, 1972, 117 pp. ($1.50)

Co-authored by the same person who wrote *The Chemical Feast,* a Ralph Nader report on the Food and Drug Administration, this book deals sharply with the baby food industry, and provides some recipes in the middle section. This is a good book for the parent who wants the complete story about commercial baby food.

The Natural Baby Food Cookbook, by M. Kenda and P. Williams, Avon, 1972, 159 pp. ($1.25)

This is a "natural" baby food book which does not mention the unnatural additives and chemicals in meat, although DDT in human milk and hydrocarbons on vegetables are reported. It is basically a cookbook for meat-eaters that starts babies eating foods a little earlier than is "natural." For example, parents are advised to offer bananas and meat once or twice a day when the baby is four and a half months old. Certainly egg enthusiasts, the authors suggest egg yolk once a day, every day, by seven months of age. Rennin (taken from calves' intestines) is called a "natural enzyme," with no mention of its source. There are no vegetarian main dish recipes in the book. However, there is a good section on the allergic child. The book ends with a strong plea for political action on the part of the parent to clean up the environment, with some practical ideas as to how to do so.

Organic Baby Food Book, by Ann Thompson, Simon and Schuster, 1973, 188 pp. ($6.95)

This is a very good cookbook for vegetarian and vegan parents, with some nutritional information included about each recipe. I recommend this as the best cookbook complement to my book. Unfortunately, it is available only in hardcover and may be currently out of print.

Your Vegetarian Baby, by Pietro Rotondi, printed by the author, no date, 80 pp. ($3.00)

Dr. Rotondi is a chiropractor who lectures on various health topics including the vegetarian life style. This is not a recipe book but rather a manual of child care and rearing for the vegetarian family. Rotondi is a little too dogmatic in his outlook for me, but I found it encouraging to read the point of view of a vegetarian doctor who obviously cares about the health of children.

Endnotes

Chapter One

[1]D. B. Jelliffe, *Infant Nutrition in the Subtropics and Tropics* (Geneva: World Health Organization Monograph Series 29, 1955), p. 122.

[2]G. T. Wrench, *The Wheel of Health* (Milwaukee: Lee Foundation for Nutritional Research, 1954), p. 48.

[3]George Ohsawa, *Zen Macrobiotics* (Oroville, CA: Ohsawa Foundation, 1971), p. 40.

[4]Vic Sussman, *Vegetarian Alternative* (Emmaus: Rodale Press, 1978), p. 115. Reprinted from *The Vegetarian Alternative* © 1978 by Victor Stephan Sussman. Permission granted by Rodale Press, Inc., Emmaus, PA 18049.

[5]Ohsawa, p. 73.

[6]*Ibid.*, p. 80

[7]*Ibid.*, p. 82.

[8]Sally DeVore and Thelma White, *The Appetites of Man* (New York: Doubleday, 1978), p. 16.

[9]Jeliffe, p. 7.

[10]*Ibid.*, p. 122.

[11]Indian Council of Medical Research, *Studies on Weaning and Supplementary Foods* (New Delhi: Indian Council of Medical Research, 1974), p. 14.

[12]*Ibid.*, p. 27.

[13]*Ibid.*, p. 30.

[14]*Ibid.*, p. 159.

[15]*Ibid.*, p. 137.

[16]*Ibid.*, p. 2

[17]*Ibid.*, preface.

[18]Louise Hagler, *Farm Vegetarian Cookbook* (Tennessee: Book Publishing Co., 1978), p. 5.

[19]Dr. Clara M. Davis, "Results of the Self-Selection of Diets by Young Children," *Child and Family*, 10:3, 1971, p. 217.

Chapter Two

[1]From *A Vegetarian Diet,* © 1978 by Shirley T. Moore and Mary A. Byers, used by permission of Woodbridge Press, Santa Barbara, CA. 93111.

[2]Karen Cross Whyte, *The Original Diet* (San Francisco: Troubador Press, 1977), p. 17.

[3]Peggy Pipes, *Nutrition in Infancy and Childhood* (St. Louis: Mosby Co., 1977), p. 1.

[4]National Academy of Sciences, *Recommended Dietary Allowances* (Washington, D.C.: National Institute of Health, 1974), p. 1.

[5]Associated Press Byline (Feb. 21, 1979).

[6]"Vegetarian Times," News Byline (Oak Park, Illinois: *Vegetarian Times,* May-June, 1979), pp. 8-9.

[7]Nathaniel Altman, *Eating for Life* (Wheaton, Illinois: Theosophical Publishing House, 1977), pp. 24-30.

[8]National Academy of Sciences, p. 2.

[9]*Ibid.*, p. 86.

[10]*Ibid.*, p. 41.

[11]Frances Moore Lappe, *Diet for a Small Planet* (New York: Ballantine Books, 1975), p. 153.

[12]Laurel Robertson et al., *Laurel's Kitchen* (Petaluma, California: Nilgiri Press, 1976), p. 424.

[13]Jeliffe, p. 143.

[14]Robertson, p. 434.

[15]Quoted by permission from *Laurel's Kitchen: A Handbook for Vegetarian Cookery and Nutrition,* by Laurel Robertson, Carol Flinders, and Bronwen Godfrey, published by Nilgiri Press, Box 477, Petaluma, CA 94952, p. 436.

[16]Moore and Byers, p. 36.

[17]Robertson, et al., p. 413. Quoted by permission of authors and Nilgiri Press.

[18]Information on vitamins, minerals, and energy adapted by permission from *Nutrition Almanac* by John Kirschmann (New York: McGraw-Hill, 1979).

Chapter Three

[1]Masanobu Fukuoka, *The One-Straw Revolution* (Emmaus, PA: Rodale Press, 1978), p. x. Reprinted from *The One-Straw Revolution* © 1978 by Rodale Press, Inc., and Masanobu Fukuoka. Permission granted by Rodale Press, Inc., Emmaus, PA 18049.

[2]"Pregnancy," *Vegetarian Times,* September-October, 1978, pp 30-33.

[3]Kirschmann, p. 247.

[4]Vic Sussman, *The Vegetarian Alternative* (Emmaus, PA: Rodale Press, 1978), p. 41. Reprinted from *The Vegetarian Alternative* © 1978 by Victor Stephan Sussman. Permission granted by Rodale Press, Inc., Emmaus, PA 18049.

Chapter Four

[1]Fukuoka, p. 139. Reprinted from *The One-Straw Revolution* © 1978 by Rodale Press, Inc., and Masanobu Fukuoka. Permission granted by Rodale Press, Inc., Emmaus, PA 18049.

[2]Christine Ripault, *Children's Gastronomique* (New York: Crown Publications, 1968), p. 372.

Chapter Five

[1]Ripault, p. 8.

[2]Fukuoka, pp. 140-141. Reprinted from *The One-Straw Revolution* © 1978 by Rodale Press, Inc., and Masanobu

Fukuoka. Permission granted by Rodale Press, Inc., Emmaus, PA 18049.

[3]Margaret Kenda and Phyllis Williams, *The Natural Baby Food Cookbook* (New York: Avon, 1972), pp 1-20.

[4]DeVore and White, p. 68.

[5]Steve Meyerowitz, "Sprout Man, Raw Foodist," *Vegetarian Times*, August, 1979, p. 26.

[6]Dick Gregory, *Natural Diet for Folks Who Eat* (New York: Harper and Row, 1973), p. 62.

Chapter Six

[1]Altman, p. 28. Quoted by permission of the publisher, The Theosophical Publishing House, Wheaton, Illinois.

[2]Herman Aihara, *Milk: A Myth of Civilization* (Oroville, CA: Ohsawa Foundation, 1977), p. 28.

[3]Frank and Rosalie Hurd, *Ten Talents* (Chisholm, Minn.: self-published by Dr. and Mrs. Frank J. Hurd, Box 86A, Rt. 1, Chisholm, Minn. 55719, 1968), p. 55.

[4]Gregory, pp 131-132.

[5]Adelle Davis, *Let's Have Healthy Children* (New York: New American Library, 1972), p. 180.

[6]Louise Hagler, p. 97.

Appendix A

[1]DeVore and White, p. 70.

[2]*Ibid.*, p. 288.

[3]*Ibid.*, p. 60.

[4]*Ibid.*, p. 280.

[5]Rudolph Ballentine, *Diet and Nutrition* (Honesdale, PA: Himalayan International Institute, 1978), pp 131-2. The address of the Himalayan International Institute is R.D. 1, Box 88, Honesdale, PA 18431.

[6]Joseph Kadans, *The Encyclopedia of Fruits, Vegetables, Nuts and Seeds* (New York: Parker Publishing Co., 1978), pp 83-84.

Bibliography

Aihara, Herman. *Milk: A Myth of Civilization*. Oroville, California: George Ohsawa Macrobiotic Foundation, 1971.

Altman, Nathaniel. *Eating for Life*. Wheaton: Theosophical Publishing House, 1977.

Altschul, Aaron. *Proteins: Their Chemistry and Politics*. New York: Basic Books, 1965.

Ballentine, Rudolph. *Diet and Nutrition*. Honesdale, PA: Himalayan International Institute, 1978.

Barkas, Janet. *The Vegetable Passion*. New York: Charles Scribner's Sons, 1975.

B-vitamins in sprouted cereal grains. *Nutrition Reviews* 1 (1943): 356.

Bircher-Benner, M. *Children's Diet Book*. New Canaan: Keats Publishing Co., 1977.

Brown, P. T., and Bergen, J. G. The dietary status of "new" vegetarians. *J. Am. Diet. Assoc.* 67 (1975):455.

Brown, P. T., and Bergan, J. G. The dietary status of practicing macrobiotics. *Food and Nutrition* 4 (1975):103-107.

Callela, John. *Cooking Naturally*. Berkeley: And/Or Press, 1978.

Crosby, William. Can a vegetarian be well nourished? JAMA 233 (1975):898.

Davis, Adelle. *Let's Have Healthy Children*. New York: Harcourt Brace Jovanovich, 1972.

Davis, Clara M. Results of the self-selection of diets by young children. *Child and Family* 10 (1971):210.

Deadman, Peter, and Betteridge, Karen. *Nature's Foods*. New York: Samuel Weisner, 1977.

Dean, R. F. A. *Plant Proteins in Child Feeding*. London: Medical Research Council, 1953.

de Bairacli-Levy, Juliette. *Nature's Children*. New York: Schocken Books, 1971.

DeVore, Sally, and White, Thelma. *The Appetites of Man*. New York: Doubleday, 1978.

Dwyer, J. T., et al. Preschoolers on alternate life-style diets. *J. Diet. Assoc.* 72 (1978):264.

Dwyer, J. T., et al. Risk of nutritional rickets among vegetarian children. *Am. J. Dis. Chil.* 123 (1979):134.

Elwood, P. C. Bread and other foods of plant origin as a source of iron. *Medical Research Council Epidemiological Research Unit* 24 (1965):112.

Erhard, R. New vegetarians. *Nutrition Today* (Nov.-Dec. 1973).

Finberg, L. Multiple nutritional deficiencies and vegetarian rickets. *Am. J. Dis. Chil.* 133 (1979):129.

Fish, Mary Bayley. *Baby Gourmet Cookbook*. San Francisco: Determined Productions, 1978.

Fomon, Samuel. *Infant Nutrition. Second Edition*. Philadelphia: W. B. Saunders, 1974.

Fomon, Samuel. *Nutritional Disorders of Children*. New York: Department of Health, Education and Welfare, 1977.

Food and Nutrition Board of the Division of Biological Sciences, National Research Council. Vegetarian diets. National Academy of Science, 1974.

Fukuoka, Masanobu. *The One-Straw Revolution*. Emmaus: Rodale Press, 1978.

Gesell, Arnold, and Ilg, Frances. *Feeding Behavior of Infants*. New York: J. B. Lippincott, 1937.

Gregory, Dick. *Natural Diet for Folks Who Eat.* New York: Harper and Row, 1973.

Gunther, Mavis, *Infant Feeding.* Chicago: Henry Regnery Co., 1970.

Hagler, Louise, ed. *The Farm Vegetarian Cookbook.* Summertown: Book Publishing Co., 1978.

Hardinge, M., and Stare, F. Nutritional studies of vegetarians. *J. Clin. Nutrition 2* (1954):73.

Hatfield, A. K. *How to Help Your Child Eat Right.* Washington, D.C.: Acropolis Books, 1978.

Hur, Robin. The facts about vitamin B-12. *Vegetarian World* (June-Aug. 1978).

Jelliffe, D. B. *Infant Nutrition in the Subtropics and Tropics.* Geneva: World Health Organization, 1955.

Jelliffe, Derrick, and Patrice, E. F. An overview of vegetarian diets. *Am. J. Clin. Nutr.* 24   (1977):1013.

Kadans, Joseph. *Encyclopedia of Fruits, Vegetables, Nuts and Seeds.* West Nyack: Parker Publishing Co., 1973.

Kardjati, Maria Sri. Protein quality of rice-soya bean and rice-green gram mixtures. *Nutrition Reports International* 13 (1976):463.

Kenda, Margaret and Williams, Phyllis. *The Natural Baby Food Cookbook.* New York: Avon Books, 1972.

Kervran, Louis. *Biological Transmutations.* Brooklyn: Swan House Publishing Co., 1972.

Kinderlehrer, Jane. *The Art of Cooking with Love and Wheat Germ.* Emmaus: Rodale Press, 1977.

Kirschmann, John, ed. *Nutrition Almanac.* New York: McGraw-Hill, 1979.

Kulvinskas, Viktoras. *Sprouts for the Love of Every Body.* Wethersfield, Conn.: Omango 'D Press, 1978.

Lane, D. E. The nutrition of twins on a vegetable diet during pregnancy, the nursing period and infancy. Am. J. Dis. Chil. 42 (1931):1384.

Lane, D. E., and Bosshardt, F. H. Nutrition of children on a mixed and on a vegetable diet. *Am. J. Dis. Chil.* 40 (1930):285.

Lansky, Vicki. *Feed Me, I'm Yours.* New York: Bantam Books, 1977.

Lappe, Frances Moore. *Diet for a Small Planet.* New York: Ballantine Books, 1975.

Larson, Gena. *Better Food for Better Babies.* New Canaan: Keats Publishing Co., 1972.

Lawson, Donna, and Conlon, Jean. *Superbaby Cookbook.* New York: MacMillan, 1971.

Lozy, M. Calculation of amino acid requirements. *Am. J. Clin. Nutr.* 28 (1975):1052.

Marqueles, Jane, and Kaufman. *The Healthy Family Cookbook.* New York: Harper and Row, 1974.

Marx, Jean. Botulism in Infants. *Science* 201 (1978):799-801.

Mason, Diane. Kids vs. vegetables: How to win the war. *American Baby* Sept. 1978:59.

McDonald, Linda. *Baby's Recipe Book.* Cleveland: C and K Publishing Co., 1972.

McDonald, Linda. *Instant Babyfood.* Pasadena: Oaklawn Press, 1977.

MacKenzie, David. *Goat Husbandry.* New York: Transatlantic Arts, 1975.

Meyerowitz, Steve. Sprout man, raw foodist. *Vegetarian Times* 30 (1979):26.

Moore, Shirley, and Byers, Mary. *A Vegetarian Diet.* Santa Barbara: Woodbridge Press, 1978.

Morris, Melinda. *The First Baby Food Cookbook.* New York: Grosset and Dunlap, 1972.

Ms. Natural. The problems of breastfeeding. *Vegetarian Times* 28 (1978).

National Academy of Science. *Recommended Dietary Allowances.* Washington, D.C.: National Institute of Health, 1974.

Ohsawa, George. *Zen Macrobiotics*. Oroville, California: George Ohsawa Macrobiotic Foundation, 1965.

Pacey, Arnold. *Gardening for Better Nutrition*. London: Intermediate Technology Publications, 1978.

Payne, Alma. *The Baby Food Book*. Boston: Little, Brown and Co., 1977.

Pierce, Pamela. Pregnancy and diet. *Vegetarian Times*, Sept.-Oct., 1978:30.

Pipes, Peggy. *Nutrition in Infancy and Childhood*. St. Louis: C. V. Mosby Co., 1977.

Rahatgi, Krishawudha et al. Effect of germination on vitamin B_{12} values of pulses. *J. Nutrition* 56 (1955):403-408.

Report cites B_{12} deficiency in strict vegetarian milk: Press jumps on it. *Vegetarian Times* 28 (1978):8.

Ripault, Christine. *Children's Gastronomique*. New York: Crown Publishers, 1968.

Robertson, Laurel, et al. *Laurel's Kitchen*. Petaluma, California: Nilgiri Press, 1976.

Robson, J. R. K. Food faddism. *Pediat. Clin. N. A.* 24 (1977):189-201.

Robson, J. R. K., et al. Zen macrobiotic dietary problems in infancy. *Pediatrics* 53 (1974):326.

Rogers, Florence K. *Another Little Mouth to Feed*. New York: Simon and Schuster, 1973.

Rotondi, Pietro. *Your Vegetarian Baby*. Hollywood: Pietro Rotondi, no date.

Safe vegetarian diets for children. *Pediat. Clin. N. A.* 24 (1977):203

Seifrit, E. Changes in beliefs and food practices in pregnancy. *J. Amer. Diet. Assoc.* 39 (1961):455.

Shull, M., et al. Velocities of growth in vegetarian preschool children. *Pediatrics* 60 (1977):410.

Smith, N., and Rios, E. Iron metabolism and iron deficiency in infancy and childhood. In Schulman, I., ed. *Advances in*

Pediatrics. Chicago: Yearbook Medical Publishers, 1974.

Spock, Benjamin. *Baby and Child Care.* New York: Pocket Books, 1977.

Subbulakshmi, G., et al. Effect of germination on the carbohydrates, proteins, trypsin inhibitor, amylase inhibitor and hemagglutinin in horsegram and mothbean. *Nutrition Reports International* 13 (1976):19.

Sussman, Vic. *The Vegetarian Alternative.* Emmaus: Rodale Press, 1978.

Thompson, Ann. *Organic Baby Food Cookbook.* New York: Simon and Schuster, 1973.

Turner, Mary, and Turner, James. *Making Your Own Baby Food.* New York: Bantam Books, 1972.

Trahms, C., and Feeney, M. Evaluation of diet and growth of vegan, vegetarian and non-vegetarian preschool children. *Fed. Proc.* 33 (1974):675.

Vegan child seen shorter, lighter than others. *Pediatric News* 4 (1977):2.

Vegetarian diets. *Am. J. Clin. Nutr.* 27 (1974):1095-6.

Whipple, Dorothy. *Dynamics of Development: Euthenic Pediatrics.* New York: McGraw-Hill, 1966.

Whyte, Karen Cross. *The Original Diet.* San Francisco: Troubador Press, 1977.

Wigmore, Ann. *Healthy Children Nature's Way.* Boston: Hippocrates Health Institute, no date.

World Health Organization. Nutrition in pregnancy and lactation. *Technical Reprint Series 302,* 1965.

Wrench, G. T. *The Wheel of Health.* Milwaukee: Lee Foundation for Nutritional Research, 1954.

Zmora, E., et al. Multiple nutritional deficiencies in infants from a strict vegetarian community. *Am. J. Dis. Chil.* 133 (1979):141.

Index